++

Forecasting
Financial Benefits of
Human Resource Development

+++

Richard A. Swanson
Deane B. Gradous

+++++++++++++++++++++++++++++++++++++++

Forecasting
Financial Benefits of
Human Resource Development

Jossey-Bass Publishers

San Francisco • London • 1988

FORECASTING FINANCIAL BENEFITS OF HUMAN RESOURCE DEVELOPMENT
by Richard A. Swanson and Deane B. Gradous

Copyright © 1988 by: Jossey-Bass Inc., Publishers
350 Sansome Street
San Francisco, California 94104

&

Jossey-Bass Limited
28 Banner Street
London EC1Y 8QE

Library of Congress Cataloging-in-Publication Data

Swanson, Richard A., date.
    Forecasting financial benefits of human resource
development.

    (The Jossey-Bass management series)
    Bibliography: p.
    Includes index.
    1. Manpower planning—Cost effectiveness.
I. Gradous, Deane B., date.   II. Title.
III. Series.
HF5549.5.M3S88   1988   658.3'01   88-42802
ISBN 1-55542-112-1 (alk. paper)

Manufactured in the United States of America

The paper in this book meets the guidelines for
permanence and durability of the Committee on
Production Guidelines for Book Longevity of the
Council on Library Resources.

JACKET DESIGN BY WILLI BAUM

FIRST EDITION

Code 8844

✝✝✝✝✝✝✝✝✝✝✝✝✝✝✝✝✝✝✝✝✝✝✝✝✝✝✝✝✝✝✝✝✝✝

The Jossey-Bass
Management Series

Consulting Editors
Human Resources

Leonard Nadler
Zeace Nadler
College Park, Maryland

✛✛✛✛✛✛✛✛✛✛✛✛✛✛✛✛✛✛✛✛✛✛✛✛✛✛✛✛✛✛✛✛✛✛✛✛

Contents

++

Figures, Tables, and Exhibits

Figures

Exhibits

Table

++

Preface

Until recently, many managers viewed human resource development (HRD) departments as supportive to the organization but dispensable. However, new expectations in business and industry have forced a change in these views. Today's managers realize that the way they manage and develop human resources can be the key to organizational success. They now know that they need to work in partnership with their HRD departments to achieve the performance goals of their organizations. For HRD to succeed in this new role, managers and HRD professionals must devote serious attention to up-front planning for the costs and financial benefits that can be expected from investments in HRD.

Making decisions about developing human resources is rarely easy. The complexities of people and the systems in which they work, as well as the constant challenge to promote organizational change, can overwhelm the most rational and conscientious of decision makers. Because so many managers in so many organizations have sought additional help with managing change of people and systems, the HRD field has grown at a phenomenal rate. Now, as never before, HRD is in a position to influence management's decisions about programs for organizational development. Also, now as never before, HRD is being held accountable for results. The purpose of this book is to describe and illustrate a model for forecasting the benefits that HRD can contribute to organizations.

Cognitive scientists have demonstrated over and over something that most of us already know: we humans have only a limited ability to juggle large quantities of information in our heads. When the complexity of the data we are interested in exceeds our capacities, we grab a pencil and a piece of paper to help us think. The worksheets in this book are intended to help you think. Forecasting the financial benefits of HRD is easier if you have a model and a method. Your goal is to analyze HRD data so that you and management can compare the financial benefits of one HRD program with those of another. What HRD decision makers have needed for a long time is a tool to reduce the complexities of choosing among alternative investments in HRD.

Genesis

Over a decade ago, the senior author listened intently to Gil Cullen, who was then manager of training and development for the Johns-Manville Corporation, as he spoke of his frustration over not having the financial tools he needed to convince top management that HRD was a sound investment. After many years of experience, Cullen had come to believe that *responsible* HRD programs yielded performance results that paid back far more to the company than they cost. At that time, Cullen and Swanson planned to execute a series of cost-benefit studies, with the goal of establishing a decision rule that for every dollar an organization spent on HRD, it could expect to gain as much or more in return. This rule, they reasoned, could then become an unquestioned part of the culture of the company—just like so many other unspoken and unquestioned decision rules on which management relies. As they progressed toward their goal, the partners became even more convinced that approval for essential HRD programs depends on whether management expects them to result in positive financial returns for the organization.

In the early 1980s, a renaissance in HRD gave us the incentive to think some more about employing HRD as an investment in organizational performance. About the same time, many writers also began to report cost-benefit analyses of HRD programs. But these writers did not address the investment dilemmas faced by managers at the program level of HRD. We believe that any competent HRD professional can do a postprogram cost-benefit analysis—difficult though it is to do well. But postprogram analysis comes far too late in the HRD process to be useful for most decision-making purposes. We believe that what the HRD profession needs is a method for forecasting the costs and benefits *before* choosing to implement a program.

How Will This Book Help You?

HRD people tend to underestimate the power of simple economic tools. The HRD financial forecasting method is a planning tool that allows you to assure yourself and others that you are making solid contributions to the strategic goals and the profits of your organization. The financial forecasting method is not an intellectual exercise. Its purpose is to help you make better decisions. Many HRD professionals prefer to work at the tactical level of planning. Perhaps you are one of them—especially if designing programs is what you entered the field to do. All too frequently, though, HRD people forget about using strategic thinking, about finding other options, and about deciding between alternative programs. They forget about doing the analytical work that really pays off—forecasting the financial benefits of HRD.

This is a book to use while you learn the forecasting method and later, as a source of models for forecasting financial information for a variety of HRD programs. Many of the case examples in this book are based on our work in the private and public sectors— in industry, business, and government. Some of the cases were created for teaching purposes. This book will show you how to

- Consider the perspective of management and the decision makers in your organization
- Join them in partnership to work toward the goals and strategic plans of the organization
- Meet management's expectations for accountability
- Use a set of worksheets to find benefits or contributions that HRD brings to the organization
- Assign dollar values to both hard and soft data
- Calculate return-on-investment ratios, as well as bottom-line contributions to earnings and to the viability of the organization
- Compare investments in human capital with one another and

with investments in capital assets or work systems designed to improve performance
- Communicate with decision makers

Who Should Read This Book?

Our intended audience includes general managers, HRD managers and staff, consultants to business and the public sector, and personnel administrators. Those who teach in the fields of management, training and development, psychology, and personnel may find the text useful for building skills in financial forecasting of HRD programs.

Overview of the Contents

The text is built around the financial forecasting model. The three steps of the model are presented systematically in Chapters Three, Five, and Seven. Sample cases in Chapters Four, Six, and Eight demonstrate how the model and the method can be used in a variety of situations. The worksheets provided will help you organize the data and jog your thinking so no important data are left out of the benefit calculation.

Chapter One sets the stage for using the model. Through many examples, we show that you have little need to *sell* an HRD program to management. When your proposal is accompanied by a forecast of the financial benefit the program will bring to the organization, the program will sell itself.

In Chapter Two, we explode four powerful myths about HRD and suggest that HRD professionals replace these myths with hard economic thinking. "No need, no benefit" is a tough but essential rule for HRD benefit forecasting. The prerequisite for realizing an economic benefit from any HRD program is that it be linked to a real performance need. Only those of us who have proven the worth of our programs time and again can get away with presenting proposals for faddish or luxury programs. Regrettably, many experienced HRD professionals have yet to demonstrate that their contributions add value to their organization. They regularly risk their careers when they present plans for attractive but nonessential HRD activities to decision makers in their organizations. You need not join their ranks.

Chapter Three is the heart of the book. In this chapter, we carefully walk you through the process of gathering data for completing the Performance Value Worksheet. The first part of the chapter is devoted to filling out the top half of the worksheet. Every line on the worksheet is examined for its purpose and for the kinds of thinking needed to gather the appropriate information. We offer advice about where in your organization to locate the necessary information. If a type of performance is valued by the organization, somebody can tell you what that value is.

The second part of Chapter Three is devoted to learning how to calculate the value to your organization of the *performance* that will result from HRD programs. Cases and graphs are included to show you how to apply the method.

Chapter Four is the first of three chapters devoted to five cases designed to show how the forecasting method can be applied in a variety of situations. The cases describe manufacturing, service, and public-sector organizations. In Chapter Four the performance values of programs in each of these organizations are analyzed. An organization development program and a management development program are also analyzed. Each of the cases includes a completed performance value worksheet and a critique and an explanation of the method used to complete the worksheet.

Chapter Five provides a framework for calculating the probable costs of an HRD program. Most HRD professionals and decision makers believe that they understand program costs better—and that costs are much easier to discover—than performance value. This is often the case, but many HRD people do not know where to locate cost information in their organizations. Nor do many know the level of accuracy needed for forecasting and appropriate decision making. Contrary to what many authors on the economics of HRD would have us believe, precision of cost figures is not the issue in forecasting. Ballpark figures are usually sufficient. In Chapter Five you will find a standard cost sheet to help in gathering and listing the typical costs incurred in every phase of your HRD programs.

In Chapter Six, we again examine the cases presented in Chapter Four. This time, the emphasis is on costs. For each case we show you what kinds of costs will be incurred and where each should be entered on the cost sheet. The goal is not to analyze each line item, but to include all major program costs and thus reach a close estimate of the total cost of a proposed program. We provide a customized cost sheet, along with an in-depth description of how to forecast costs for one case.

Chapter Seven contains a brief summary of how to calculate the benefits of an HRD program and how to compare alternative investments. We also explain how to present your forecast to management. When you, the forecaster, begin to appreciate the high levels of real value that HRD brings to your organization, your next task is to understand the decision maker's "window of believability." In most organizations factors other than economics will enter into HRD decision making. But this does not make forecasting the financial benefit any less useful. Once the economic benefit, or lack of benefit, is known, it can be weighed along with other important decision criteria, such as timeliness.

In Chapter Eight, we complete the five cases begun in Chapter Four and continued in Chapter Six by providing the Benefit Analysis Worksheet for each case and our rationale for choosing and presenting to management the financial benefit forecast for one or more of the available options. Each case highlights a different lesson in HRD decision making.

Finally, because practice with feedback is essential to learning the method, in Chapter Nine we offer a variety of practice exercises to increase your understanding of the model. Completed worksheets following each case provide feedback on your ability to analyze each case situation. Here you will also find blank worksheet forms to copy and use in completing the exercises. After closely examining the sample cases and completing the exercises, you will be ready to complete forecasts in your organization with confidence.

Acknowledgments

Support for our ideas came from Brian P. Murphy, president of HRD Department, Inc., and formerly director of human resource planning and development for Onan Corporation. Murphy served as cheerleader and benefactor to a new program of research at the University of Minnesota on forecasting the financial benefits of HRD. This book, along with several other research publications, was the result.

Two other people contributed significantly to the research that underlies this book. Gary D. Geroy and Catherine M. Sleezer worked with the senior author to develop and validate the formulas and to establish their usefulness to HRD practitioners. Geroy, assistant professor of training and development at Pennsylvania State University, continues a program of research related to HRD strategic planning. Sleezer is a consultant and researcher who works with organizations in implementing their HRD programs. Both have generously shared with us their work on many of the case studies in this book and their ideas about the practical applications of the methods in real-life settings. Many other individuals and organizations have contributed in a variety of ways to this work. They include Gil Cullen, Farhood Heidary, Ralph E. Long, Northern States Power Company; Mitchell E. Kusy, Jr., IDS/ American Express, Inc.; Nancy R. Mosier, Arthur Andersen & Co.; Barbara L. Parker, Process Management Institute; Robert J. Prifrel, Control Data Corporation; Gary R. Sisson, Paradigm Corporation; James H. Sleezer; and the Department of Vocational and Technical Education at the University of Minnesota.

We hope that you will find this book easy to read, accurate, complete, and useful. Moreover, we hope that it will give you a new view of your role in your organization and the tools that can help you fulfill it.

August 1988   Richard A. Swanson
                                                St. Paul, Minnesota

                                                Deane B. Gradous
                                                Wayzata, Minnesota

To
Mary E. Swanson
and
Frederick J. Gradous

The Authors

Richard A. Swanson is professor and director of the Training and Development Research Center of the Department of Vocational and Technical Education at the University of Minnesota. Swanson received his Ed.D. in industrial education from the University of Illinois in 1968. He earned his B.A. and M.A. degrees in industrial education (in 1964 and 1965, respectively) from Trenton State College.

Swanson has received numerous awards, including the Bowling Green State University Faculty Research Award, the G. Harold Silvius Outstanding Scholarly Publication Award, and the Outstanding Trainer of Trainers Award from the Minnesota Chapter of the American Society for Training and Development. He has served as editor of both the *Performance & Instruction Journal* and the *Journal of Industrial Teacher Education,* and as president of the National Association of Industrial and Technical Teacher Educators. Before joining the University of Minnesota faculty, Swanson was professor and coordinator of graduate studies in industrial technology at the University of Northern Iowa, 1978-79, and professor and director of graduate studies in career and technology education at Bowling Green State University, 1968-1978. With Deane B. Gradous, he has coauthored *Performance at Work* (1986) and edited *Adapting Human Resources to Organizational Changes* (1987). In addition, he is the author of more than 100 publications on the topic of education for work. He is currently doing research on evaluating HRD programs and organization-wide change.

Deane B. Gradous is a human resource development consultant in Wayzata, Minnesota. She received her B.A. from Valparaiso University in business and English (1955) and her M.B.A. from the College of St. Thomas in St. Paul, Minnesota (1977). She has worked as a researcher, consultant, and trainer for many organizations. With Richard Swanson, she coauthored *Performance at Work,* which received the Outstanding Instructional Communication Award of 1987 from the National Society for Performance and Instruction. Gradous has also written and edited many books for internal use in organizations and is currently researching the elements of responsible management development.

+++++++++++++++++++++++++++++++++++

Forecasting
Financial Benefits of
Human Resource Development

1
++

Developing a Bottom-Line
Orientation for HRD

Financial benefit forecasting is a before-the-fact method for selecting the best among alternative human resource development (HRD) programs. The method is similar to the analytical methods that managers use for deciding which products to develop and which equipment to purchase, as well as whether or not to expand or relocate facilities. If making decisions about major investments in organizational assets deserves thorough analysis, then making decisions about HRD investments merits the same thorough analysis. Most would agree that HRD programs represent major outlays of organizational resources. For this reason, decision makers require information about an HRD program's expected impact on organizational performance. Lacking sufficient information, decision makers could fail to support just those HRD programs that have the greatest potential for producing significant benefits for the organization. For this and other business reasons, financial benefit forecasting is potentially the most effective skill that the HRD professional can acquire. If the results of HRD programs are forecast in terms that organization leaders can understand, the HRD professional will likely gain top management's enthusiastic commitment. HRD and management will become true partners in seeking and reaching organizational objectives. Work performance is the key, and valuing that performance in dollars and cents is the method.

We get excited every time such a partnership evolves. Recently Walt Godfrey, HRD manager of a local corporation, wanted to consult with us about his upcoming meeting with the chief executive officer and two vice-presidents of his corporation. Believe it or not, in his six years as HRD manager, Walt had never seriously read his company's annual report, let alone scheduled a meeting with anybody to discuss how the HRD department could contribute to corporate earnings. Two months previous to our meeting, Walt had asked us for all the information we could give him on forecasting the financial benefit of HRD. He read and learned. His transformation was quick. Walt was crossing the threshold to becoming a true business partner with his company, and he wanted some last-minute reassurance. Walt's proposal to management was solid. He had identified a critical performance need of the organization. He had spelled out a realistic performance goal. He had forecast the financial benefits, and he had clearly documented them. We were not at all surprised, later in the week, to hear that management had approved Walt's business proposal.

In many struggling companies, executives have come to view HRD as an essential business function, the purpose of which is to increase corporate earnings through cost-effective organization development and employee training. HRD professionals want to exert more influence in their organizations, and management wants them to make greater contributions. The efforts of those who can handle the pressure are paying off in increased responsibility for HRD departments and greater earnings for the organization. As regional, national, and worldwide competition becomes more and more intense, corporate leaders will increasingly recognize that employees are resources that must be maintained and developed. Managers are learning that investing in HRD is as important as investing in new technologies. They are finding that it does an organization little good to invest in sophisticated systems if employees can neither understand these systems nor operate the new technologies within their work environments. High-level individual, work-group, and organizational performances are the key, and responsible HRD programs focus on increasing those performances.

The following demands for human resource development that will have to be met in the next decade illustrate the size of the challenge:

- Orienting and training twenty-six million new employees
- Developing millions of current workers who need to learn new skills
- Developing three to four million managers

In 1985, the American Society for Training and Development estimated that American employers annually spend between $30 and $50 billion on programs to develop their employees (Carnevale, 1983). When the value of the work time that employees expend in HRD is included in these estimates, the cost of HRD doubles. In the 1984 supplement to the January 1983 *Current Population Survey,* the U.S. government indicated that about thirty-six million, or approximately 33 percent of all employed people, received either formal company training or informal on-the-job training. Given such a high level of corporate concern and investment, it is no wonder that organizations want their HRD professionals to think like business people—not like teachers, counselors, or record keepers.

When decision makers decide to spend large sums of money on HRD, they seek to evaluate HRD program options much as they evaluate other large investments, that is, on the basis of financial returns to the organization. It therefore follows that employee development efforts, for the most part, should be tied to the profit-making goals and performance plans of the organization, whether it be profit making or in the public sector. Wherever underperforming employees reduce organization productivity, all will suffer. The public will be poorly served. Market share will be lost. The organization's earnings will be diminished. For these and other reasons, HRD decisions made outside of the performance-profit frame of reference are open to question. But if decisions are made within this frame of reference, HRD becomes an important means for meeting the goals of the organization, whether they are for profit or for service.

HRD professionals can contribute to changing technologies at work, can help people perform new job tasks, and can overcome the disaffection that workers at all levels feel between themselves and their organization. HRD professionals can be prepared to prove to management that their programs will raise organizational performance. Such proof is developed by calculating accurate, meaningful base-line measures of performance and relating any expected increases in these measures to specific HRD programs. To demonstrate the relationships between HRD and improvements in performance or profit, HRD professionals must learn to use financial analysis methods similar to those used for making capital-investment decisions. Remember, work performance—individual or group—is the key, and forecasting benefits of changing work performance is the subject of this book.

Bottom-Line Orientation

Depreciation schedules, returns on investments, and payback periods have been used for decades for calculating investments in capital goods. Decision makers use these valuable tools selectively because they have not had an equivalent forecasting tool for analyzing potential investments in human capital. As a consequence of the lack of a decision method, most decision makers have failed to consider fully the financial consequences of their HRD policies and decisions. Typically, managers fall back on using only cost questions when they budget for HRD: "How much will it cost?" "How much did we spend last year?" "How much do we want to spend this year?"

Because they apply only cost questions to their HRD programs, most decision makers fail to recognize HRD's genuine contributions to the organization. Inevitably, they view the company's HRD department as a costly burden rather than as the means for obtaining higher levels of valuable work performance. We should not be surprised to find managers in organizations of all sizes and types making tough HRD decisions without benefit of a financial forecasting tool. The following examples are typical:

• A medium-size manufacturing company producing electronic circuit boards earned steady profits. Even with high rates of employee turnover and rejection of product, the company continued to make money. The management group had never considered the possibility of investing in HRD. Thus, spending any money at all on HRD would be a significant departure from normal company practice. When a consultant proposed that the company invest $20,000 in training ten assembly workers, management wondered at the extravagance. The management group was unaware that in just forty days this investment could return over $200,000.

• Recently, the executive vice-presidents of a Fortune 100 company instituted a whole new approach to developing their work force. Their stable, experienced, and productive work force had always learned how to do their jobs through trial and error. A thorough cost-benefit analysis showed that significant increases in employee work performance could be expected to result from a formal program of supervisory development. Eventually, the financial benefits actually realized from four new HRD programs more than matched the forecast benefits. Not surprisingly, the executive vice-presidents have chosen to institute HRD investments right along with their capital investments throughout the organization.

• In yet another instance, a corporate manager of HRD had to choose one program from among several optional programs designed to develop new work attitudes and new initiatives in the current work force. The proposed HRD program could be produced by an in-house staff, by several HRD vendors, or by two public educational institutions. Which one should be chosen to do the project?

Decision makers face a major difficulty. Their understanding of the economics of HRD as a major factor in increasing the value of human resources in their organizations is limited. Attention to the economics of specific HRD programs is rare. Searches through the literature on organization development and employee training yield little on the subject of forecasting the financial benefits of HRD activities. Lacking appropriate analysis tools, decision makers attempt to apply to HRD the cost-benefit analysis tools that they have traditionally applied to capital investments, despite the fact that human competence does not depreciate on a scheduled basis. In fact, human knowledge, attitudes, and skills can be expected to grow. Human development often works like a chain reaction; get good people started in the right direction, and they will tend to continue on that path. Such growth may even be contagious.

Playing by Corporate Rules

Companies exist to make profits through competent employee work performances. By establishing goals and strategies, decision makers determine what individual, group, or organizational work performances will be pursued. At the level of strategic planning, executives may invest in improving organizational performance through HRD or through such other measures as marketing, new equipment purchases, expanded sales regions, or mergers and acquisitions. HRD managers carefully allocate scarce organizational resources (financial or human) with the expectation of attaining their goals. But the very idea of being held financially accountable for HRD investment decisions can be threatening. How do they know what is the "right" decision when investing in human resources? In the past, HRD managers turned to traditional training and development evaluation methods. Evaluation of learning is not new. Educational institutions have been evaluating student learning for decades. But the business perspective on evaluating worker performance and other HRD outcomes is different. In business and industry, HRD outcomes are measured in dollars and cents. In the public sector, HRD outcomes are measured in terms of service. The business perspective on evaluating worker learning is different because here decision makers focus on the results of applying the expertise rather than on the expertise itself. Such applications of expertise lead to improved performance and to increased organizational prestige or earnings.

HRD may be viewed as a business process that converts inputs into outputs. Employees are the inputs. Employee work performances that contribute to the goals of the organization are the outputs. Economic analysis of HRD can be used to decide whether or not to invest in an HRD program and whether to continue or discontinue an HRD program. It can also be used to decide between different vendors' HRD program offerings and between various HRD program methods for achieving the same performance goals. Finally, it can help determine which potential participant groups will achieve the highest or most valuable performance goals. HRD programs are usually evaluated after organizational resources have been committed and consumed. Such after-the-fact evaluation offers hindsight, but it usually contributes little toward increasing decision makers' confidence about returns on HRD investments to be made in the future. Financial forecasting is needed. The financial benefit forecasting method is an essential tool for analyzing and choosing among optional HRD expenditures in organizations. It makes it possible to answer an important economic question.

What Is the Gain?

It is important for you, the HRD professional, to understand the relationship between what you do and the financial benefits you produce for your company. With HRD financial benefit forecasting, you have in hand a tool that will allow you to connect a sound performance need with a sound HRD solution to that need.

With this tool you, the HRD manager, will be ready and willing to be held accountable for the programs of your HRD department. If and when you are asked about what you do, you will have ample evidence of the value of your HRD activities—that is, if you begin now to use the tool to analyze performance problems and the benefits that result from your HRD solutions to those problems.

With HRD financial benefit forecasting, you have the means to show decision makers in your company, and yourself, how to value HRD. You and the executive decision makers have the means to help people grow and to make strategic choices about the HRD department. Moreover, you and the executive decision makers have the means to evaluate potential solutions to organizational problems that may have been overlooked or undervalued.

As you will note throughout your reading of this book, we believe that "responsible," structured HRD generally results in the greatest benefit for the organization. Structured HRD sometimes is proposed as a solution to a non-HRD performance need or as a weak solution for a performance problem better solved through management action. In such less responsible applications of HRD, the financial forecasting benefit method will yield forecasts that are borderline or negative—exactly the kind of information you need to keep you from making the big mistake of investing in structured HRD that is incapable of improving organizational performance.

2

++

HRD Financial
Forecasting Basics

For most HRD professionals, forecasting the financial benefits of
HRD programs represents a new area of expertise. It possibly also
represents a new role for the HRD department in implementing
organizational strategy. The purpose of this chapter is to develop
an understanding of the role that financial forecasting can have in
planning for HRD benefits in any organization and to introduce the
financial forecasting model. The following case is based on a real-
world situation.

The HRD Fantasy

Gregg Southerland's HRD department didn't make it
through the reorganization intact. A confident Director of HRD,
Gregg had a smooth-running operation. Only recently, the HRD
department's executive advisory committee had evaluated and
approved a new corporate executive development program. Gregg
seemed to be doing all that could be expected of a director of HRD
in a Fortune 100 corporation.

A capital-intensive organization, his company employed a
relatively small work force. Those employees who were selected for
participation in HRD programs immediately found themselves on
the "fast track," receiving quick promotions and generous rewards
for their efforts. The HRD department enjoyed being a part of and
promoting the good times. Years ago, Gregg purposefully had
chosen to maintain a supportive role and a "corporate perk"
atmosphere for his HRD department. He handled his leadership

role with a blend of dignity and celebration, and his department had been successful for some time.

Then the economy took a sudden nose dive, and Gregg's once seemingly strong and impervious department went down with it. Decades of easy growth had caused many of the company's operations to become soft and overgrown. Gregg's department, as a promoter of good times, had little to offer his company when it encountered difficult times. In less than six months, Gregg's highly polished staff of ten was reduced to Gregg and one administrative assistant. During the corporatewide reduction in the work force, it was not clear to top management that the HRD department could address the fundamental issues of the business. And in such times the fundamentals are all that matter.

Even if the HRD department had focused on the economics of the business, it probably would have been somewhat reduced in size. Without exception, all departments had experienced cuts in staff, but what hurt the most was that the goals of the HRD department weren't really given serious consideration when the cuts were made. Gregg had believed all along that his department was making important contributions to the company. Now he suddenly had to come face-to-face with management's perception of his department's minimal worth to the company. Ironically, just two months before, Gregg had emphatically rejected an offer from an expert consultant in financial forecasting to help him and his staff talk to top management about the economics of the HRD department. Gregg confidently reported to the consultant that HRD received wonderful support from top management. Further, he thought that discussion about the financial contributions of HRD was not necessary. When the HRD department finally did hear about its worth from top management, it was too late. Gregg's perception of top management's support for the HRD department had been a fantasy.

Exploding HRD Myths

A number of value-laden myths have entered the HRD profession. These myths may be partially the result of HRD's having taken on too many "it feels good" goals without performing thorough needs assessments and work analyses to back up their HRD programs. Some myths that have currency in HRD include:

1. Social pressure is the basis of HRD.
2. Managers don't care about HRD.
3. HRD costs too much.
4. You can't quantify the benefits of HRD.

These myths should be exploded. Hard economic thinking and even harder planning are what is needed, not mythology. We believe that HRD professionals should be business persons first and HRD specialists second. The four HRD myths will evaporate when the transition to thorough performance needs assessment and professional accountability becomes commonplace.

Myth 1: Social Pressure Is the Basis of HRD. A quick look around the corporate world will reveal hiring programs, training programs, and other HRD programs that were put into place because "everyone else is doing it." Perhaps some companies get trapped in this game in the same way that some parents get trapped by their children's wanting things because other children have them. Perhaps some HRD managers have used such childish threats with management as "the company across the street has one and so should we."

We have heard talk within the HRD profession about "employee rights to development," along with statements that "HRD is a corporate perk." This kind of rhetoric seems to suggest that social pressure is the basis of HRD. But isn't it interesting that HRD professionals in those organizations that strongly support HRD programs rarely, if ever, use social pressure? Most organizational decision makers who actively support HRD view it in terms of anticipating economic gains or averting economic risks.

Myth 2: Most Managers Do Not Care About HRD. Because so few managers defend their HRD departments, ask for their help, or sing their praises, HRD professionals could easily come to believe that this myth must be true. Simultaneously, these same managers consult with others in the company about such important issues as developing work-force expertise, motivation, and aptitude, and how to design work so people can be more effective in their jobs.

Never make the mistake of confusing management's caring about HRD issues with their caring about the HRD department. Furthermore, we urge you to acknowledge that the hardworking managers in your company put themselves on the line every day. Right or wrong, most managers will rely on what they believe to be their best and most trusted sources of help. Even though your HRD department may not have earned such "best" or "trusted" labels, this does not mean that most managers don't care about HRD. Managers do care about HRD. But to be a "best" and "trusted" source of know-how requires that the HRD department have a believable forecasting and evaluation system.

Myth 3: HRD Costs Too Much. Good HRD generally costs a fair amount of money. Most of the worthwhile projects that go on in an organization cost a fair amount of money. Usually management decides to spend available dollars on the equipment, services, and projects that will give it the best return on its investment. Whenever something must be purchased that apparently will have little effect on the business, management will request the one with the lowest price.

The following example will have a familiar ring: If low-quality mailing envelopes will do the job, management tends to say, "Get them as cheaply as you can." If these inexpensive envelopes later stick together or will not feed through the postage machine, or if they make the organization look tacky in the eyes of customers, management then will tend to say, "Stop buying such junk." Conversely, if the most expensive envelopes are the kind that seal automatically and thus increase output, or if they catch the attention of potential customers and bring increased sales, management will tend to say, "Get a good price if you can, but we want the best."

Cost figures by themselves are irrelevant. Reviewing HRD costs without also reviewing the associated benefits is not smart. Analyzing what you get for your money *is* smart. What most HRD managers fail to realize is that organizational decision makers usually focus only on HRD costs. When they lack information about the economic benefits of HRD, many decision makers decide consciously or unconsciously that a proposed HRD program is just another HRD program—just as an envelope is only an envelope. "So get the cheapest one."

Myth 4: You Cannot Quantify the Benefits of HRD. Listening to people find excuses why something cannot be done is always interesting. Rationalizing that the benefits of HRD cannot be quantified has kept the HRD profession in the dark ages of organizational performance. Do you suppose that management knows how many products it will sell next year? Of course not. If it knew the correct figures ahead of time, it would make exactly that many products. But because management does not know precisely how many products it will sell, it gathers the best estimates it can find and makes its decision without the satisfaction of knowing it is right. This process takes intelligence and guts—not perfection. Likewise, a little more intelligence and a lot more guts on the part of HRD professionals will explode this last myth.

There is a strong possibility that all four of these myths have arisen from inside the HRD profession. If decision makers have also learned these HRD myths, they probably learned them from HRD people. Executives, as masters of change and opportunity, have the right to expect HRD departments to join them in their struggle to achieve quality and profitability. Most decision makers are not enemies of HRD. They want to be business partners and to reap the added value that HRD can provide to the organization. All four HRD myths stand in the way of this partnership.

No Need—No Benefit

The real pressure for HRD activity will come as the result of identifying critical performance needs. Good needs assessments are essential to fully utilizing the financial benefit forecasting method. A thorough performance needs analysis can be conducted by management, by HRD staff, or by a consultant. Identifying less-than-obvious corporate needs requires gathering critical data from corporate production records, employees, customers, and the like. Even the more obvious needs, such as the need for communication skills, would benefit from a thorough performance needs analysis. Analysis will ensure that an HRD program closely fits the development needs of a specific executive group in a specific corporation. Too often, HRD programs, expensive or not, fail to deliver what is needed. They deliver what they promise and still miss the need. Because conducting good performance needs assessments is essential to creating value through HRD, we suggest that readers consult the very helpful works by Kaufman (1986) and Mager (1970).

A major practical issue in most organizations is how to distinguish between wants and needs. What managers want is not always what they need. Needs are critical conditions that organizations must meet in order to achieve their missions. The benefit-need relationship is important. Wants are not so important. The critical HRD skill is to be able to work with decision makers to discover genuine organizational performance needs and to convince them that they want what they need. This goal is best accomplished by working in partnership with managers rather than by making high-pressure attempts to sell faddish HRD programs.

HRD *wants* are easy to identify and to sell to decision makers: "What do you want?" "Is this what I heard you ask for?" "Okay then, here is the program you wanted." Filling such wants is a relatively safe process. But in doing so, it is easy to ignore your organization's mission, performance goals, and performance deficiencies. The outcome of an HRD program that addresses an organizational need is valuable to the extent that it satisfies that need. Some HRD analysts believe that organizational needs are more complex than wants. We don't necessarily agree. Satisfying needs is just riskier. And with greater risk comes the potential for greater gains—for the HRD department and for the organization.

The outcome of a particular HRD program is valuable only if it is connected to an organizational performance need. A high-cost HRD program does not always result in a performance gain, while a low-cost HRD program may result in a large performance gain. Determining the critical performance to be attained and its value to the organization should precede the step of analyzing the costs of the HRD program.

Conducting a thorough performance needs assessment is

important, but the question when is enough, enough? will inevitably be raised. Enough investigation is enough when HRD professionals feel comfortable with the answers to the following questions:

- Have we identified a need for performance that is important to management?
- Will the HRD program positively influence that performance?
- Can we deliver a high-quality HRD program?
- Will the right people in the organization participate in the HRD program?

It goes without saying that forecasting the financial benefits of various HRD program options will help all concerned along the path to making better decisions. An important component of any performance needs assessment is the HRD financial benefit proposal to be presented to management.

Connecting Needs with Benefits

The outcomes of HRD programs are valuable only to the extent that they are connected to specific organizational performance needs. Additionally, HRD programs must have integrity and quality or they will not deliver the expected benefits. The basic economic issue of investing in HRD is the same as that of investing in other forms of capital. The question is one of return on investment. Will investments in people net the kinds of returns—and the magnitude of returns—that the organization is seeking? Strategic opportunities, issues, costs, and profits are basically the same for investing in HRD as they are for investing in capital assets. In a competitive market, the organization must fully utilize its human resources to maximize its bottom-line results. In the nonprofit or government worlds, the organization must use its human resources to provide more or better service with limited resources.

Decision makers have three possible options with which to address an organizational need for competent human resources. The first option is to retain the existing work group and initiate retraining or other HRD programs to develop the competent workers they need. The second option is to fire the existing work group and acquire a new one that possesses the requisite knowledge and skills or other desired characteristics. With this option, the issues of supply and demand for labor are similar to those for any other market commodity. The third option is to try to foresee the implications of current and future economic, social, and political forces, to consider the limited available organizational strategies, and then to choose whether to go out of business, seek out a more favorable labor market, or automate.

Our bias is in the direction of the first option. Evidence can be gathered to indicate whether the various work performances in the organization, especially the poorer performances, can be improved through HRD programs. Such evidence is gathered through the aforementioned performance needs assessment process. After this assessment has identified which specific work performances may be addressed wholly or in part by HRD programs, the task of forecasting HRD costs and benefits becomes an essential element of the decision-making process. Before exploring the specifics of this task, however, it is important to gain a historical perspective on HRD investments.

HRD Role Shift

Recent shifts in world economics have made severe inroads into the former pre-eminence of American industries and businesses. This is especially true for low-skill, labor-intensive industries. The transfer of what were once American jobs to offshore locations has triggered numerous social and political reactions. These reactions have ranged from instituting protectionist legislation to negotiating new labor contracts that mandate job protection and retraining. Offsetting the loss of American jobs are the short-lived advantages held by those relatively few organizations with new technologies.

Today, as never before, new and evolving technologies can be speedily replicated. New applications for current technologies are discovered at an ever accelerating rate. An organization decides to invest in new technologies when it perceives that all its competitors in a given market have access to the same technologies for the same relative cost. A failure to invest in appropriate capital assets and technologies can therefore quickly lead to the loss of an organization's competitive position in the marketplace. At the same time, investment in new technology alone cannot ensure economic success. The critical competitive edge in many organizations lies in the efficiency and effectiveness with which its workers implement and maintain the corporate technologies. Two organizational variables that influence efficiency and effectiveness of performance are the attributes of the organizations themselves and the skills and knowledge of their workers. Viewed from this perspective, HRD quickly becomes the priority investment option because it will lead to desired worker, work-group, or organizational performances that will, in turn, yield a competitive return on investment. Although the notion that new technologies and employee skills can be purchased as commodities may be disliked by some, such is the economic reality of some very successful organizations.

Cost-Only View of HRD

Human capital has been defined as an individual's capacity to produce goods and services (Carnevale, 1983). Individuals, firms, and societies invest in people—in human capital—to enhance and maintain individual, work-group, organizational, and societal capabilities. The challenge has been extended to HRD to assist organizations in carrying out their missons. HRD departments have achieved a high degree of visibility in recent years. An organization's ability to respond to rapid market and technological changes depends a great deal on the capacity of its personnel to assimilate new knowledge and skills. Directed change, however small, is seldom accomplished without cost. This fact is true whether the change is a matter of investing in capital assets or in human resource development. Assessing whether costly HRD programs are wasteful frills or essential strategies is possible only if their relative effectiveness is known. Before addressing the issue of costs and effectiveness, however, we will review some of the more common ways to think about costs and HRD.

Unplanned, unstructured HRD has long been considered the most cost effective of HRD programs. Why is this? Because most managers do not associate costs with organizational changes that evolve without benefit of planning or with changes that are gradually forced upon an organization by external pressures. The "hassles" associated with change are frequently accepted by managers as the normal inefficiences of doing business. In contrast, most managers tend to view *planned* HRD programs as incurring costs, costs that must be accounted for in their operating budgets. Such thinking leads to the question: If an organization can attain desired changes in performance without incurring any perceived costs, why should management bother to invest in HRD? What these managers fail to consider is that any less-than-optimal quantity of valued performance in an organization is in some real sense a loss to that organization. For example, poorly made products and poorly performed services can be thought of as economic losses to the organization. Such thinking is a departure from the cost-only perspective that is more usual in making decisions about HRD programs.

The three most common cost questions in reference to HRD programs are: "How much does it cost?" "How much did we spend last year?" "How much do we want to spend this year?" This customary perspective yields very different decisions than does the perspective of analyzing the benefits to be gained from each HRD investment.

Benefits Aspect of Cost-Benefit Analysis

Cost-benefit analysis usually presumes that, given the cost of an investment and the value of the resulting change, the benefit can be determined. Current management thinking about the benefits to be derived from investments is rooted in traditional models for investing in capital assets. The benefit of any capital investment is generally expressed as the value of achieving some additional organizational output over some period of time. Alternatively, it may be expressed as a ratio of the value of some additional output to the cost needed to achieve that output. Most capital investment models take into account such factors as depreciation and inflation.

In this traditional approach to thinking about expected investment benefits, two ideas are evident. First, the direct output to be derived from the investment is the focus of the analysis. If a machine is to be purchased, the decision maker looks at its potential output. If a building is planned, the decision maker looks at its potential contribution to organizational output. Second is the notion that the change that results from the investment will have value to the organization.

The cost-benefit analysis of HRD programs that is described in this book honors much of this traditional thinking about capital investment, but it entails a few major departures from the normal method of analysis. One departure is the need to recognize that the value of a human being does not depreciate. HRD investments actually constitute a relatively stable form of value added to the organization. A second departure is that the focus of the analysis of benefits expected to result from HRD activities may be quite broad. Many HRD programs focus on providing or enhancing the technical skills and knowledge that will allow individuals or groups to produce more effectively or efficiently on the job. Quite often, however, the impact of newly acquired skills and knowledge will be of an abstract nature, such that it can best be anticipated as desired changes in the work performances of the peers or the subordinates of the people who actually participate in the HRD activity. For example, the performance of a work group may be expected to improve as the direct result of new skills to be learned when their supervisor enrolls in an HRD program. Or perhaps it is a drop in worker turnover caused by a disagreeable management style that is the expected performance result of an organizational development intervention with the plant management group.

A third departure from standard investment models is the period of time on which the analysis of future benefits focuses. The analysis of benefit from HRD is limited to the *period* during which several alternative HRD programs could be implemented and bring about the same change in performance. As we have stated, conducting a thorough performance needs assessment is important. A needs assessment will help to identify any performance discrepancies that may have HRD solutions. It also will help in identifying alternative

HRD program options that could achieve the same desired change in performance. If several optional HRD programs can be expected to yield the same end-performance results, then the key variable in the HRD financial forecasting model will be the length of time each program takes to achieve the desired performance (Figure 1).

The fourth and most significant departure from standard investment thinking is the difficulty of defining the specific benefit to be derived from a particular HRD investment. In traditional capital investment models, the benefit is the value of the additional products or services produced. In the HRD benefit-forecasting model, the specific benefit to be derived is the value of future changes in performance after the costs to achieve that change are deducted. This idea suggests that cost-benefit analysis of HRD programs requires a third component, namely the value of the additional performance or the change in performance that is expected. This third component in the HRD benefit forecast model is called the *performance value*.

Figure 1. Performance-Time Graph.

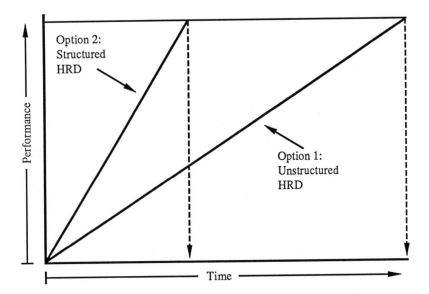

Performance Value

Improvements in organizational performance can best be effected by investing in capital assets, by investing in human capital through programs of selection and training, or by investing in some integrated combination of capital assets and HRD. Thus, changing worker or work-group performance to fill an organizational need is only one strategy for organization survival.

In many organizational situations, the desired performance change is an *increase* in quantity of a valued output or activity. For example, the goal of HRD in a research organization may be to increase the number of patents granted per researcher. In another instance, the desired performance may be a *decrease* in quantity of an unwanted output or activity. For example, the goal of an HRD program in a chain of hotels might be to reduce the number of regular customers lost.

When looking at performances that will change as a result of HRD programs, the analyst must focus on the base-line performance level, which is the measure of performance prior to the HRD program. The desired performance level is the level of performance expected to occur as a direct result of the HRD program. In some cases an HRD program may begin before the performance of the target group or organization begins. An orientation program for new workers is an example. But an HRD program could also begin whenever the target group or organization performs at a level lower than the desired performance goal. This would be the usual situation whenever a system or a procedure or the structure of the organization is to be changed. For example, HRD activities may focus on team building and negotiating leadership roles in newly structured work groups. In this situation, the aim of the HRD program might be to reach a specified performance goal by developing efficient communications, clarifying decision-making responsibilities, and retaining valued workers. The gain in performance from the base-line level to the desired level will be valued and included in the HRD cost-benefit analysis.

HRD Benefit-Forecasting Model

Several models for assessing the financial benefit of HRD programs have been available to decision makers for some time

(Mosier, 1986). The three most commonly used models are return on investment, benefit-cost ratio, and payback period. These models appeal to decision makers because they are familiar. Many managers have grown accustomed to using such models to assess the value of investing in capital assets. Some managers have been applying these investment models to the task of evaluating the actual results of HRD programs, but not to forecasting the expected results.

One unknown variable in forecasting the results of an HRD program may account for the lack of forecasting in organizations. That variable is the length of time that the returns from one program option will be effective in comparison with the length of time that all other available options will be effective. Another problem with using financial models in forecasting the benefits of HRD is the difficulty in assigning a dollar value to qualitative benefits. Any way we figure them, the numbers we use to represent the costs and benefits of HRD to the organization may never provide a complete picture of the value of a proposed program. There may be many nonquantitative outcomes that should, but will not, be considered. These include such "ceremonial" effects of HRD as (1) employee recognition, (2) the company's reputation for caring about its workers, and (3) the general quality of life at work. Given these constraints, the goal of conducting an objective cost-benefit analysis of an HRD program can become an interesting challenge.

In the following chapters we provide the analyst with strategies for quantifying these difficult qualitative dimensions. The model presented does not view benefits as the value of the change in performance but rather as the value of the change in performance minus the costs incurred to achieve that change. The model takes into account existing performance levels and any changes in performance that may be brought about as a result of both HRD and non-HRD activities.

The basic HRD benefit-forecasting model that will be presented and described in the following chapters includes methods for determining monetary values for the following components: (1) the *performance value* to result from the HRD program, (2) the *cost* of the HRD program, and (3) the *benefit* resulting from the HRD program. The HRD benefit-forecasting model is simplicity itself:

$$\frac{\text{Performance Value} - \text{Cost}}{\text{Benefit}}$$

Forecasting the costs of HRD can be quite a challenge. But identifying and valuing the change in performance that is expected to result from the HRD program are even more challenging.

Forecasting Versus Evaluation

It is relatively easy to evaluate the effectiveness of an HRD program once the effort has been completed. But it is often quite difficult to evaluate and choose the best among several HRD program options for achieving a desired performance goal. It may be even more difficult to choose between several HRD program options, and several non-HRD options.

Evaluation examines the *effects* of a program (Phillips, 1983; Parker, 1986). Forecasting develops economic data for *making choices* between HRD program options and between HRD and non-HRD options. The financial forecasting method supports forward-looking, decision-making processes. The goal is to make better HRD decisions before investing in programs, rather than to wait to evaluate HRD after the investments have been made.

The forecasting task is performed by the analyst as the last step in the performance needs assessment process. It is an essential part of making proposals to management. While this text concentrates on forecasting the benefits to be derived from HRD programs, the methods are equally powerful for evaluating the actual effects of HRD programs.

The usefulness of any forecasting model in the decision-making process is dependent on its capacity for enhancing human capabilities for coping with quantities of data. When they are forecasting the benefits of proposed HRD programs, decision makers are challenged by the overwhelming availability of so-called soft data. Soft data, which are generally not highly valued by decision makers, tend to have the following characteristics:

- Difficult to measure or quantify directly
- Difficult to assign dollar values to

- Based on subjective criteria
- Less credible as performance measures than hard data
- Usually behaviorally oriented

Conversely, although they can be the more difficult to obtain, hard data are highly valued by decision makers because they appear to be accurate and precise. Hard data have the following characteristics:

- Easy to measure, quantitative
- Relatively easy to assign dollar values to
- Based on objective criteria
- Often already being used as measures of organizational performance
- Credible in the eyes of management

The importance of using hard data for forecasting purposes becomes obvious when we review the various levels at which evaluation takes place and the type of data upon which decision makers willingly stake their program decisions—and their reputations. There are three levels of evaluation—satisfaction, learning, and performance (Swanson and Sleezer, 1987). Performance evaluation focuses either on measures that report changes in desired organizational outcomes or on the costs and benefits of the completed program. The financial forecasting model presented here is designed to be used to forecast the dollar benefits of HRD programs before they are implemented. Chapters Three through Eight explain how the model addresses these hard-data issues and how the forecaster can simply and systematically work through a prescribed process to identify the expected performance value, as well as the costs and benefits, associated with each HRD program option.

A New View of HRD's Role

The economics of HRD are reflected in (1) profit, (2) strategy, and (3) forecasting. Let's briefly examine each of these areas.

Profit. The old saying that business is in the business of making money reflects a fundamental value that HRD people must accept and support. If the HRD department cannot contribute to returns on investment, management must then try to minimize the costs associated with HRD activities. Thus, the HRD professional should either be tuned into the business of making money or be prepared to keep expenses to an absolute minimum.

Strategy. Many articles and books have been written and many speeches have been given about developing business strategy. The strategic planning models that are generally available to management typically cover aspects of the organization's mission, strategy, and human resources, as well as the societal context in which the organization operates, including the economic, political, and cultural forces that impinge on it (Tichy, 1982). Understanding organizations and the hodgepodge context in which they must operate represents a new role for HRD people. Further, such matters are complex. Gearing up to support the business strategy of an organization means that HRD professionals must become increasingly cognizant of the economic factors that are involved in making strategic decisions.

Forecasting. Tea leaves and crystal balls too often come to mind when we hear the term *forecaster*. To us, the best forecasters are those with good data. The most effective forecasters make timely forecasts. Right here, however, is where the greatest forecasting difficulty enters the picture. In general, forecasts are made at a point in time when decision makers do not have all the necessary data. Furthermore, obtaining the needed data almost precludes delivering a timely forecast. Risk taking is an essential element in melding available HRD data into the business timetable. Using an effective HRD financial forecasting model and method can increase one's confidence in the data and thus provide an element of security for the forecaster.

Summary

We have made a case for the economic analysis of HRD activities and for forecasting the financial benefits of HRD. In doing so, we have looked at the myths that stand in the way, the important relationships between performance need and financial benefit, and the basic financial concepts dictating a new organizational role for HRD.

We discussed the three components of the financial forecasting model—performance value, cost, and benefit—in detail. The next step is to learn how to use the method and how to apply it. The three components of the model supply the organizers for the next six chapters—Chapters Three and Four (performance value analysis), Chapters Five and Six (cost analysis), and Chapters Seven and Eight (benefit analysis). In Chapter Nine we offer several practice exercises so you can achieve confidence in forecasting the benefits of HRD in any organization. We chose to present the performance value information first for several reasons. Most important, we want you to begin the forecasting process with an entrepreneurial mind-set rather than concentrating on the burden of HRD costs. Valuing performance is also the most challenging task. Further, we believe that the beginning forecaster can transfer more of the knowledge gained from performance value to cost analysis, rather than the reverse. Most authors on the economics of HRD have approached the subject from the cost perspective first. They have then discussed the financial value of HRD in a few short paragraphs or dismissed it as being impossible to derive. We know otherwise.

3

++

Calculating the Dollar Value
of Performance Improvements

Performance is the key to financial benefit analysis. All work in organizations should be aimed at meeting performance goals, such as contributing to profit, increasing product or service quality, retaining valued employees, or remaining in the good graces of regulators. Performance goals are essential to the long-term viability of organizations—and to the jobs they sustain. Responsible HRD programs, those that influence positive changes related to specific performance goals, can be measured in dollars and cents. This chapter provides the information you will need to forecast the value of such performance.

Remember, what gets measured gets done (Peters, 1987). If HRD professionals don't measure their successes, others will do the measuring for them. And the measuring rods that other people use tend to underestimate HRD's real contributions. With financial benefit analysis, HRD professionals can determine and communicate their contributions to the organization—just as Jim Forrestor recently learned to do.

Jim's Situation

Jim Forrestor walked with confidence into the regular Friday morning meeting of his senior management team. He was well prepared. A few hours of examining production reports and scrap records had yielded the figures he sought. Now, here he was, ready to show that the new job guides his department had prepared for the operators of the B-14 machines had already returned an astonishing $12 for every $1 invested in them. While the other members of the group acknowledged the good results of the B-14 Job-Guide Program, Jim remembered how hard he had fought to hire an expensive HRD consultant to help write the job guides. Without a doubt, Sheila Karter was worth more than her large consulting fee. By making a careful work analysis and exercising her excellent writing skills, she had created a number of precise and correct job guides. Then, too, she had used her skill in working with people to ensure that the new guides would be well received by the operators. For the last eight months, the operators have checked their job guides *before* adjusting their machines for each new job lot—instead of *after* making a short run of unacceptable pieces. Jim's calculations of the worth of these new work behaviors to the organization were as follows:

Performance Value (increased product + decreased scrap)	$169,700
Cost of B-14 Job-Guide Program	–18,000
Benefit	$151,700

Talking Management's Language

Jim Forrestor has learned how to communicate in the language of the senior management team, and all HRD professionals have a similar opportunity. In the past, many of them have talked easily and well about such issues as keeping valued customers and aligning reward systems with desired performances. Those are important goals. But these HRD professionals have failed to talk about programs in the language that top management understands best—dollars and cents.

The challenge is to convert HRD jargon into the language that is most easily understood by management, the language of financial gains and benefits. Once this challenge is met, HRD professionals will truly be prepared to answer management's question, "What does HRD actually do for the company?"

But before we can talk fluently about financial benefits, we must first learn to calculate the *value of performance*. Performance gains, whether they be expressed in terms of (1) timeliness, (2) quantity, or (3) quality features of products and services, generally represent money in the bank.

Let's clarify where we stand on this challenge to establish the performance value of work. We believe that with a little bit of thought and some careful investigation, the value of any work performance in any organization can be calculated. That is, *if the work contributes to the performance goals of the company, it can be valued in dollars and cents.* Whenever HRD programs are directed toward reaching the performance goals of the organization by accomplishing work that is valued in dollars and cents, the odds are greatly increased that HRD will be taken very seriously in that organization.

An Approach to Performance Value Analysis

To calculate the value of improved work performance, you need to gather four pieces of information:

- *Unit* of work performance. Some clearly definable unit of work performance is always present in any task or job role. If it cannot be identified, perhaps the HRD program is not worth considering.
- *Performance levels.* Both the existing level of performance and the target level of performance to be reached in a designated period of time must be determined.
- *Value* of each unit. Each defined unit of work performance must be valued in dollars and cents.
- *Performance value.* Performance value is obtained by multiplying the value of one unit of work performance times the total number of units that can be attributed to the HRD program.

The method for determining each piece of information on the Performance Value Worksheet will be explained later in this chapter. For now, the following discussion will help you understand how each piece of information is used in performance value analysis.

What Are Units of Work Performance? A decision must be made about what the *unit* of expected work performance is. The objective is to relate this unit directly to the original performance needs assessment and to the work performance that will result from the HRD program. For example, units expected to result from the HRD program could be customer service features, insurance forms processed, machines maintained, employees counseled, or customers retained.

When we attempt to determine the unit of work performance, the issue of separating wants from needs becomes important. For example, the chief executive officer may demand that he see less paper flow at headquarters. Yes, some measurable unit of paper flow could then be defined. But too much paper flow is probably only a symptom of the real problem. A good performance needs assessment in this instance would have revealed that the way the organization is currently structured has led to unclear lines of responsibility and decision-making authority, which in turn has caused a spate of excessive and inefficient communications about relatively unimportant matters. Because paper flow is just a symptom of the real problem, it should *not* be the unit of work performance to be improved by the HRD program. The unit of performance to be measured might better be the timeliness of critical decisions.

What Is the Performance Level? Performance level is the amount of something accomplished. Calculating the performance value requires that the beginning performance level be determined and the target performance level be predicted. The current performance level is the amount of performance accomplished at the beginning of the HRD program. The target performance level is the amount of performance expected at the end of the HRD program.

For example, an HRD program to institute a new reward system in a large financial organization was expected to decrease the number of managers who left the firm. To avoid working the performance value calculations in negative numbers, the HRD consultant reviewed the company's records and discovered that 180 managers had been retained each year. He predicted that as a result of implementing his HRD program, 186 managers would be retained in the coming year. In this example, the beginning performance level is 180 and the target level, or performance goal, is 186. The forecast performance goal of six additional retained managers represents value to the organization. Accurately forecasting performance levels requires analysis skills and confidence in the quality of HRD programs.

Even small gains in performance are worth a great deal when they are multiplied over time or for many workers. For example, let's suppose that an organization employs about 200 managers and about 10 percent of them leave every year. In positive terms, the organization has a 90 percent retention rate. A needs assessment clearly identifies that ongoing, inexpert supervisory behavior is causing managerial resentment and turnover. The HRD department believes it can partly remedy this situation. A promise to increase the proportion of managers retained to 100 percent would be considered quite unrealistic. No organization can expect to totally satisfy all its employees. Furthermore, good managers may be offered outside job opportunities that the organization is not willing to match. A conservative performance goal, one that is reachable given the situation and the resources dedicated to the task, will be set. In this situation, promising a 93 percent retention rate for managers is realistic. Three percent, or six managers, may seem like a small gain in performance, but when this number is multiplied by the dollar value of one retained manager, the performance value gain is significant. Performance goals, besides being accurate, must be realistic, obtainable, and significant.

What Is the Value of a Performance Unit? The financial *value* of one unit of work performance must also be determined. Each unit of performance, whether it is a lowered level of employee turnover or a higher level of products produced, is worth something to the organization. Accountants or other fiscal managers can generally assist the forecaster in estimating this value by checking company records. In Acme Company, for example, the current finished inventory of 6,000 widgets is carried on the books at $12,000. At this rate, one widget—one performance unit—is worth $2. The accountant agrees that this is a conservative valuation.

In a similar vein, the value of processing additional insurance forms will probably be known to the manager of a claims department. Let's say that 18,000 forms are processed each week by forty-five people at a cost of $45,000. The company goal is to achieve this performance with forty people—a savings of $5,000 per week. In consultation with department managers, the HRD manager develops a new work design for the claims-processing task. This new work design makes the expected performance level possible. The performance value of achieving this goal is 28 cents per form, $5,040 per week, or about $131,000 over the next twenty-six weeks. The company reaps the rewards of the performance gain, and the HRD department earns the respect of management.

We return to our previous example on managerial turnover. It is usually fairly easy for a company to place a dollar value on employee turnover. We are certain that you could find out what it costs your organization to replace an employee at any level in your organization. Replacing good employees who leave is usually a very costly matter. Instituting a new supervisory training and action program to eliminate even a small portion of this turnover expense can represent a significant financial gain for the organization.

What Is the Performance Value? Performance value is the financial worth of the number of performance units that result from an HRD program. The performance value of an HRD program is calculated by multiplying the total number of units expected to result from the program times the dollar value of one unit.

To illustrate this, let's continue with the turnover case. The HRD manager estimated that six additional managers per year would be retained as a result of the HRD program. Six managers times the organization's average turnover expense of $75,000 per manager is a performance value of $450,000. In this case, both the number of *units* (six) and the financial *value* of each unit ($75,000) were conservative estimates.

This brief discussion of the four pieces of information needed for valuing work performance, (1) unit, (2) performance levels, (3) unit value, and (4) performance value, has set the stage for an in-depth look at the process of forecasting the performance value.

Computing the Performance Value

As illustrated in Chapter Two, the benefit-forecasting model has three elements—the performance value, the cost, and the benefit. Of the three, determining the performance value requires the most extensive calculations. Even so, *the method is orderly, not very complex, and one that HRD people have used successfully time and time again.* The foregoing description of the elements required to conduct the analysis has revealed a small portion of the method for forecasting the value of performance. To become a competent forecaster, you need to know more and you need to have additional tools. The remainder of this chapter covers the process for developing forecasting data and provides a worksheet for forecasting the *performance values* expected to result from proposed HRD programs. In a similar way, the following chapters will cover program *costs* and program *benefits*.

While you are engaged in the forecasting process, it is important that you keep two perspectives in mind. One perspective is that of the *venture capitalist,* the other, that of the *accountant.* We believe your perspective ought to be like that of the venture capitalist who tries to estimate the gains from a particular course of action, relies on common sense, and is willing to take risks. Venture capitalists do not worry unnecessarily about small details. Their main activity is big-picture planning. Forecasting the financial benefits of HRD programs is the same sort of big-picture activity.

The Performance Value Worksheet (Exhibit 1) can assist you in your big-picture thinking. The worksheet will guide you through the process. The worksheet asks the questions, and you provide the answers. Spaces on the form allow you to record your estimated figures. The worksheet assumes that you understand the forecasting process. It uses the four pieces of information we have already talked about. Fortunately, the completed worksheet can be easily interpreted by decision makers who have little or no knowledge of the process you used to get your figures. The remainder of this chapter is dedicated to a more detailed description of the logic to use in filling out each line of the worksheet. At first glance, the worksheet may appear somewhat formidable. We can tell you now that your responses to items *a* through *g* will provide you with all the information you need to determine the performance value expected to result from your proposed HRD program. You might find it useful to keep a copy of the worksheet before you as you read the next several pages.

When beginning, be sure that you record the HRD program name, your name, and the date in the worksheet heading. Don't fail to perform this step because you will probably need the information later. The next information called for on the worksheet heading is the names of all the HRD program options that you are considering. We offer two pieces of advice as you explore the important question about HRD program options. Be sure to

- Connect your HRD program to the performance goal that was identified during the performance needs assessment
- Consider the full range of HRD options with which to address the performance goal before choosing two to four of the most reasonable ones

Performance needs assessments are critical to implementing responsible HRD programs. Needs assessments help in identifying the basic human performances on which business goals depend. Even given an excellent needs assessment, one that includes specific performance goals, HRD managers sometimes use the wrong criteria to select HRD programs. They do this because of the biases of top managers, their own prior experience with available HRD programs, or an infatuation with certain HRD program delivery methods. But each of these reasons should remain secondary to the main question as to whether or not the program is capable of producing the desired work performance.

Forecasting the financial benefits of an HRD program connects the performance needs assessment to the HRD program in a dramatic fashion. The performance need, the program to meet that need, and the dollar value of the resulting performance ought to be clearly related. When the performance need and the HRD program cannot be clearly and directly connected and when no dollar value can be attached to the performance goal, the HRD manager should reconsider the results of the needs assessment, the possible HRD program options, or the appropriateness of HRD as a means to achieve the identified performance goal. When HRD managers deliberately raise such questions as they fill in the

Exhibit 1. Performance Value Worksheet.

Note that performance units and time units for all options must remain consistent throughout the forecast.

Program _____ Analyst _____ Date _____

Option name	1	2
Data required for calculations:		
(a) What **unit** of work performance are you measuring?	_____ unit name	_____ unit name
(b) What is the performance goal per worker/work group at the **end** of the HRD program?	___ / ___ no. units / time	___ / ___ no. units / time
(c) What is the performance per worker/work group at the **beginning** of the HRD program?	___ / ___ no. units / time	___ / ___ no. units / time
(d) What **dollar value** is assigned to each performance unit?	$ _____ / unit	$ _____ / unit
(e) What is the **development time** required to reach the expected performance level?	___ time no.	___ time no.
(f) What is the **evaluation period**? (Enter the longest time (e) of all options being considered.)	___ time no.	___ time no.
(g) How many workers/work groups will **participate** in the HRD program?	___ no. workers/groups	___ no. workers/groups

Calculations to determine net performance value:

	Option 1	Option 2
(h) Will worker/work group produce **usable units** during the HRD program? If no, enter -0-. If yes, enter known performance rate or calculate average performance rate. [(b + c)/2]	no. _____ units	no. _____ units
(i) What total units per worker/work group will be produced during the **development time**? (h x e)	_____ no. of units	_____ no. of units
(j) How many units will be produced per worker/work group during the **evaluation period**? {[(f – e) x b] + i}	_____ no. of units	_____ no. of units
(k) What will be the value of the worker's/work group's performance during the evaluation period? (j x d)	$ _____	$ _____
(l) What is the performance value gain per worker/work group? [k – (c x d x f)]	$ _____	$ _____
(m) What is the **total performance value gain** for all workers/work groups? (l x g)	$ _____	$ _____

Performance Value Worksheet, the odds of achieving harmony among need, program, and performance results are increased. Thus, as part of the decision-making process, HRD managers, designers, and program providers will need to ask themselves if they truly believe that their HRD programs will result in the specified performance goal and what evidence or logic they have to back up their claims.

To guard against routine habits of problem solving, which will often be counterproductive in finding the best HRD solutions, divergent thinking is important. For instance, one company that we worked with was so accustomed to purchasing management training from external providers and designing its own technical training that it failed to ask external providers to bid on technical training projects. On one occasion we nudged the HRD manager into procuring an external bid for a technical training program. She was shocked to discover that the external provider was willing to produce and deliver a program comparable to the proposed in-house program at an earlier date and at 70 percent of the cost. The manager realized that she had probably ignored many excellent program alternatives in the past.

Figure 2 is a useful map for thinking about a whole range of structured HRD options. The "source" axis reminds us to consider using both internal and external providers. The "type" axis reminds us to consider a variety of custom-made and off-the-shelf programs. Any proposed HRD program option will fall either into a single cell or into some combination of the cells. Program C illustrates an off-the-shelf program that was customized by a team of internal and external HRD personnel to meet the needs and style of the organization and was then delivered by internal HRD personnel.

Another important role of forecasting is to compare struc-tured HRD program options to the existing unsatisfactory situa-tion. Existing unsatisfactory situations can result from both formal (structured) or informal (unstructured) HRD programs. Remember, there is no such thing as no HRD. The existing HRD program may be unconscious, unplanned, unsystematic, and ineffective—in a word, unstructured. Even so, such unstructured HRD programs are in place. They are usually assigned no direct costs, and they

Figure 2. HRD Program Options.

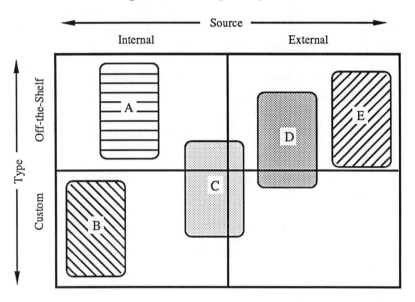

Note: A through E are examples of HRD program options.

generally bring unknown financial consequences to the organization. If an unstructured program or an unsatisfactory structured program is already in place in your organization, it cannot help but make the forecast benefits from responsible HRD program options look good. Certainly, you should use the current unsatisfactory condition as one of your program options.

Performance Description

The first major item on the worksheet (Exhibit 1) is to describe the work performance expected to result from the HRD program (item *a*). The skilled forecaster may be able to answer this question straight out. The less experienced forecaster will first need to answer a series of subquestions that begin with describing the work performance expected to result from the program, exploring the dimensions of that performance, and establishing levels of performance within those dimensions. After this preparatory step, the forecaster will then decide on the unit of performance (item *a*) to use in determining the performance value of the HRD program. In responding to these subquestions, the analyst will produce the information for the following worksheet items (Exhibit 1):

(*a*)   What unit of work performance are you measuring?

(*b*)   What is the performance goal per worker/work group at the end of the HRD program?

(*c*)   What is the performance per worker/work group at the beginning of the HRD program?

The subquestions leading to worksheet items *a*, *b*, and *c* are as follows:

(a—*Tentative*) *What unit of work performance are you measuring?*

- What is your best description of the performance resulting from the HRD program?
- Is there a unit of time associated with the work performance? If yes, what is it?
- Is there a unit of quantity associated with the work performance? If yes, what is it?
- Is there a unit of quality features associated with the work performance? If yes, what is it?

(b) *What is the performance goal per worker/work group at the end of the HRD program?*

- What is the work performance unit goal in terms of time, quantity, or quality features?
- Are performance records (time, quantity, quality features) being kept by the organization?
- Is it reasonable to record this work performance (time, quantity, quality features) in the organization?

(c) *What is the performance per worker/work group at the beginning of the HRD program?*

- Time:
- Quantity:
- Quality Features:

What reasonable alternatives will be considered for the unit of work performance?

- Time:
- Quantity:
- Quality Features:

> (a—*Final*) *What is your final decision as to the unit of work performance you will measure?*

Explanation of the Subquestions

The first subquestion asks for an *initial* statement about the work performance that will result from the HRD program. This answer is derived from the performance needs assessment. Depending on the situation, the answer could specify a very clear unit of performance that has value to the organization, or the answer could still be fuzzy and in need of further clarification. For example, a needs assessment in one large organization pointed to an excess number of lengthy and inefficient meetings. The initial work performance goal was described as "less time spent in meetings." A planned HRD program with the objective of improving skills in selecting attendees for the meetings was considered. In their performance needs assessment, however, the analysts missed the critical point that the performance goal of managers in this organization is neither attending meetings nor running shorter meetings. If this were so, participating managers, upon completion of the HRD program, would know how to run efficient meetings, and they could then comfortably return to their jobs and use the extra time for coffee, cigarettes, and idle chatter. The expected work performance in this case probably had something to do with the *timeliness* of managerial decisions, the *quantity* of work performed back on the job with the time gained from shorter meetings, or the need for significant improvement in the *quality features* of the decisions made during the meetings. To help sort out these tough questions about work performance, the subquestions probe further.

In exploring the exact nature of work performance units, the forecaster can look at three dimensions:

- Time
- Quantity
- Quality Features

Performance units in all three dimensions can ultimately be quantified. The HRD program should be aimed at measurable improvements in one or more of the dimensions.

Time is here defined as the measurable interval between two events or the period during which some activity occurs. In the workplace, performance is commonly measured in terms of time. Gains in performance time usually yield important financial consequences to the organization.

The situation at the drive-in window of a fast-food restaurant illustrates this point nicely. It was discovered that by moving the air-hose bell twenty feet ahead of the ordering point, the order taker could be on call at the moment the vehicle driver stopped at the window to place an order. This change in the workplace reduced the time to process each order by several valuable seconds. In another situation, we observed an HRD program that resulted in a four-month reduction in the amount of time it took sales personnel to learn their jobs fully. In another instance, the new-product design and setup teams learned to cut their design-to-production time in half—a highly valued outcome given their organization's competitive race to the marketplace.

Quantity is a measure of the exact amount or number of products, services, or other outcomes that result from worker or work-group performances. Quantity units are relatively easy to define and monitor in the workplace. Examples of such quantity units are the numbers of patents approved, clients served, sundaes sold, and sales earned. All three of the performance dimensions must be quantified, but the "quantity" dimension is the only one that is restricted to counting the simple, usually observable, worker or work-group outputs.

Quality features are the characteristics of products or services that meet agreed upon specifications. Some of the quality features of a product or service include design, procurement, manufacturing, marketing, sales, service, customer education, and ultimate disposition (Tribus, 1985). We know of a computer manufacturer that has a set of requirements in all these areas. The manufacturer's design specifications focus on such features as the size and capabilities of the computer. Its specifications for sales and customer education include such quality features as acceptable selling practices and a method for determining customer training needs. Because most companies compete with each other on the basis of meeting customer specifications, improvements in product or service quality features are worth dollars and cents to the company. Consequently, HRD programs that enhance product or service quality features have value to their companies.

HRD programs can be aimed at improving either *end-product* or *in-process* quality features. End-product quality features are characteristics of the final product or service. In the computer manufacturing example, an end-product quality feature would be an increase in the quality of the surface finish of the monitor, which would make it more attractive to both the distributor and the retail customer.

In-process features are characteristics that products or services have while they are being made. Organizations often determine in-process quality specifications that products and services must meet with the expectation that these, in turn, will lead to desired end-product quality features. For example, it is important to an airline that passengers feel a great deal of confidence when they fly on a commercial airline. Management expects pilots to follow prescribed preflight check-sheet procedures (in-process specifications) and to get to their destination safely (end-product specification). Common sense suggests that the forecaster should not always wait for an end-product measure to determine whether an in-process performance is valuable. If this were the case, pilots could neglect their in-process check sheets until a sufficient number of near-fatal or fatal accidents warranted a crackdown on their work performance.

As you can see, we have rather narrowly defined our dimensions of time, quantity, and quality features. Broader definitions would not be particularly useful for determining the units of work to use in forecasting the short-term financial benefits of HRD. For example, a forecaster could agonize unnecessarily over how to express the two dimensions of quantity and time. Time can be expressed in two ways: (1) numbers of units produced in a set block of time or (2) the time needed to produce each unit of performance.

Thus the performance goal could be to increase the *number* of widgets made or the *number* of counseling sessions conducted in an eight-hour day. Or the performance goal could be to decrease the *time* it takes to produce a widget or conduct a counseling session. In our drive-in window situation, the performance goal could be expressed as total number of sales during a period of time rather than as the time required for each sale.

In forecasting, the performance value is directly related to the time, quantity, or quality features of the expected units of work performance. While the forecast will focus on just one of these dimensions, the HRD manager needs to consider all three in order to achieve excellent results. If the analyst at the performance needs assessment stage were to focus on a single dimension—time, quantity, or quality features—without being aware of their interrelatedness, the organization would likely end up in trouble. We recall a bank where the customer service personnel were given incentive pay for the number of telephone calls they completed. Whenever the computers were not operating, the customer-service people told each caller only that the computer was down. They then hung up the telephone, took the next call, and added to their incentive pay. The needs of the customers were ignored. In this instance, an emphasis on quantity-only criteria led to a significant loss in important quality features.

For forecasting purposes, either time, quantity, or quality features must be chosen as the primary vehicle for valuing performance gains. At the same time, the HRD manager must remember to monitor the other two dimensions. Assessing the full range of work performance dimensions at the needs assessment stage ensures that the HRD program does not promote gains in one dimension at the expense of the other two.

To summarize our discussion of the features of time, quantity, and quality features, we offer some examples of usable performance units:

Time (focus on the period during which something happens):

- Two minutes to process a fast-food order
- Forty manufacturing hours per generator housing
- Fifty minutes per service call

Quantity (focus on numbers of things):

- Twenty circuit boards per worker per eight-hour shift
- Five employees coached per week in team-building skills
- $110,000 new-car sales per month
- 999,999 out of a 1,000,000 acceptance rate of .50″ diameter metal rings per thirty days of production

Quality Features (focus on attributes):

- A 4-point, or higher, annual satisfaction rating for hotel accommodations and service
- Five customer courtesy steps taken on 100 percent of the monthly transactions
- Ninety-five percent acceptable (pass) fruity wine bouquet per forty-hour inspection period

All the dimensions cited are positive, and represent gains that can be stated in positive numbers. While it is possible to work with negative numbers by citing absolute values, the HRD financial forecasting method requires positive values. For example, the forecaster can cite "fewer defects in a product" through its inverse, "gains in acceptable products."

Performance Levels

Thus far we have described two items on the Performance Value Worksheet (Exhibit 1) by working through the subquestions:

(*a*) What unit of performance are you measuring?
(*b*) What is the performance goal per worker/work group
at the end of the HRD program?

Item *c* on the worksheet (Exhibit 1) has to do with determining the beginning performance level in those units of work performance that are still being considered:

(*c*) What is the performance per worker/work group
at the beginning of the HRD program?

At this point all three features—time, quantity, and quality features—could still be under consideration as potential units of work performance. Here we raise a few questions about measurement and organizational record keeping. The answers will help us choose the most practical unit of work performance for a specific HRD program.

If organizational records are already being kept on a unit of work that leads to the performance goal, this unit of work will obviously be much more attractive than one on which no records are being kept. Existing records provide a basis for comparison over time and eliminate the effort and expense of setting up a special measurement scheme. Existing records are usually seen as credible and not open to manipulation. Ideally, you will find an existing record of one of the units of work performance that you have under consideration.

As a rule, organizations keep records of the work performances that are *critical* to the organization. If the proposed HRD program is truly focused on important work performances, the odds are good that records are already being kept on the performance of the responsible individuals or work group. Sources of useful records include departmental production and scrap records, accounting department figures, business plans and reports, and sales and service charts.

If appropriate records are not being kept, the next subquestion asks, Is it possible to collect and record the data? Without a system in place for keeping records of the work performance, the forecaster may need to propose one. If so, the overriding concern is that the record-keeping system be both valid and simple. For example, one forecaster settled on the simple and direct measure of new memberships as the most important unit of work performance. The organization's HRD and marketing departments were simultaneously engaged in programs designed to gain new members. A meeting of vice-presidents to decide on the *relative performance value* of the two programs was the best available means for separating out the contributions of the individual programs. This decision by upper management was credible to everyone in the organization. The unit of work performance—new members—was simple, valid, and useful.

Unit of Work Performance Decision

We have walked through the process for deciding the unit of work. We have looked at dimensions of work performance, checked out existing work performance record-keeping systems in the organization, and cited the need for credibility.

At this point, a meaningful decision can be made as to the unit of work performance that will actually be used to forecast the financial benefit of the proposed HRD program. Ultimately, this decision is easy because answers to the subquestions have either confirmed or redirected your thinking. Perhaps only one or two of the three dimensions of work performance units are left for consideration. The final choice should be based on practical concerns. Which HRD unit of work option is

- Most clearly connected to the original need?
- Easiest to implement?

Thus the harmony among need, program, and results is once again tested and confirmed in this decision.

Value of Unit of Performance

With answers to items *a*, *b*, and *c* filled in on the Performance Value Worksheet (Exhibit 1), finding the answer to item *d* is the next step:

(*d*) What dollar value is assigned to each performance unit?

This question, more than any other, intimidates forecasters. But sitting at your desk and fretting over it will not lead you to the answer. Getting up and talking to non-HRD people is generally the only realistic means of acquiring the answer. People in your organization keep numbers on almost everything. Sometimes these numbers are unknown to the people who are actually carrying out the work activity in which you are interested. Sometimes they are known only to the people who are one or two tiers above the activity in the organization.

The HRD staff members of a manufacturing company were attempting to forecast the financial benefit of training workers to operate some new machining centers. They talked to the machinists, to the supervisors, and even to the department head to get a "good number" to use in their forecast. When nothing came of their inquiries, they asked us to come by for a short conference. We did so. After listening to their frustrations, we suggested that they call the vice-president of manufacturing at home, as it was then 6:30 P.M. The vice-president had authorized the purchase of the machining centers. Within seconds he informed the HRD director that the machining centers were expected to put out $635 of product per hour. There it was. The dollar value that had been used to make the purchasing decision could now be used to make the training decision.

Our advice on assigning a dollar value to a unit of work performance falls into two categories: (1) source and (2) method. As noted above, the source is usually outside the boundary of the HRD office and within the boundary of the financial decision makers for the business or for a particular part of the business. The information you need may be on paper, or it may be in someone's head. In either case, you will likely have to access the information through non-HRD people. You will need to call, visit, and cajole department heads, accountants, and vice-presidents of sales and marketing. These people will have the information you need.

Some useful questions for locating the *sources* of the dollar value of each unit of performance include:

- Does someone in the organization already know this value?
- What manager or accountant would most likely know this value?

Once again, we urge you to note that the closer your HRD program is connected to an important performance goal of the organization, the more likely it is that you will find good sources for the requisite financial information. Thus the harmonious connection among need, program, and results is tested once again.

Obviously, you will not have to choose a method for placing a dollar value on a unit of performance if the organization has already done the job for you. Regrettably, this will not always be the case. The value may be missing, or it may be imbedded in the value of a larger unit of work, which your program only partially addresses. In such a case, you must drag out your crystal ball again and come up with an intelligent estimate. Our method for finding intelligent estimates hangs on two notions:

- *Estimating* the dollar value of each unit of performance is okay.
- The estimator must have *credibility or authority* in the organization

Remember, however, that it is the venture capitalist's view of forecasting that you are using, not the accountant's view. Estimates are acceptable. We use them all the time in making our own life decisions, and organizations use them for making very big decisions. You must learn to feel comfortable with estimating the financial worth of units of performance. To become an effective forecaster you must rely on the help of appropriate people in your organization. Clearly, if you have access to the hard numbers, use them. If not, you must estimate them. Just be sure to consult with individuals who have credibility or authority in your organization. Trade and professional journals that report the standard dollar value of units of work performance are credible sources. If such published figures are applicable to your company, use them. Do not go it alone; rely on others.

For a close look at dollar valuing we can review the situation with which Barb Johnson, director of HRD, was faced.

Barb Johnson saw a serious communication problem in the manufacturing firm for which she worked. The problem had to do with the technical language that was used by teams of design engineers, prototype/setup people, and production workers—a language called *geometric tolerancing*. In Barb's company all kinds of awkward and counterproductive work behaviors occurred because the production workers did not understand the language of geometric tolerancing. The prototype/setup people knew a little of this language, and the design engineers knew a lot. The engineers in particular were using their know-how about geometric tolerancing to get their way. Even when the engineers were, in fact, wrong, the others could not communicate on the same ground.

Barb knew that a common understanding of the language of geometric tolerancing would get the teams back on track, which in this situation would mean significant reductions in the time it took to make compromise decisions between the three levels of manufacturing. The unit of performance that was expected to result from the HRD geometric tolerancing training, therefore, was a reduction in the number of days it took to achieve compromise manufacturing decisions and a corresponding gain in the number of days of productive work. Putting a value on the days of productive work that would be gained was the most difficult estimating problem that Barb had yet encountered. Here is how she proceeded: First, she identified key people in the firm who were versed in its productivity and work system. They knew time and materials costs and could discuss such matters as the flow of products within the organization. Second, she obtained available records of average times for design, redesign, and production. She also gathered information about scrap costs and the production rates associated with part types. Third, she met with the director of manufacturing and an accountant to obtain agreement on what they thought the financial consequences of protracted decision making had been. (They identified engineering time spent on redesign and production losses during redesign period.) Fourth, she obtained agreement from the director of manufacturing that production rate was the most useful unit of performance *and* and that it was a very conservative estimate of the true financial picture. Finally, she was able to get the same decision maker to place an estimated value of $18,500 for production per eight-hour day.

Johnson now had the necessary information to answer items *a* and *d* on the Performance Value Worksheet. You, like Barb Johnson, will run into some seemingly difficult valuing situations. Always remember that you need to step outside of your office, that it is all right to make estimates, and that you should rely on others who have the credibility or authority to make decisions about unit performance values.

Time to Reach Performance Goal

An important task in comparing HRD program options is to answer worksheet item *e*, which asks about the time it takes participants to get to the performance goal:

> (*e*) What is the development time required to reach
> the expected performance level?

You will recall from Chapter Two that time differences in reaching performance goals can result in costly losses or valuable gains in productivity. Figure 3 compares structured with unstructured HRD, a situation where the gains in valued performance are relatively assured. But when you undertake to estimate the time requirements, another gut-wrenching issue surfaces: Does each option have the capability of achieving the desired performance goal. That, however, is another problem and another book. For purposes of the present discussion, we assume that the answer for each option is yes.

Once the unit of work performance has been established, the unit of time should be specified. Typical time units include hours, days, or weeks. It is wise to use whatever units of time your organization typically uses and always to keep the time units constant within the forecast. Only very unusual HRD programs would use time increments as small as minutes or as large as months. Sometimes HRD programs will have a short classroom session or retreat followed by one or more structured activities in the workplace. When follow-up activities are part of the HRD program, the forecaster will probably use weeks rather than hours as the preferred unit.

Selecting the unit of time is the easy part. The more difficult part is estimating the time it will take to achieve the desired performance goal for each HRD program option. Here are two bits of down-home advice:

- Call it as you see it.
- Move on.

Figure 3. Performance-Time Graph Showing the Sources of Some of the Items on the Performance Value Worksheet.

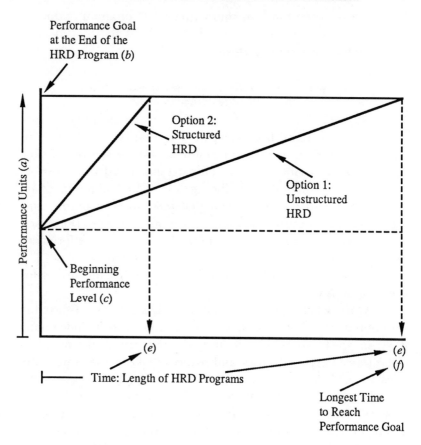

Have you ever umpired a baseball game? Your first time is a funny experience. If you don't call the pitches, the players and the fans will. You soon learn that the worst thing is to *not* call the pitches as they come at you. In some ways being a forecaster is like being an umpire. You never know for sure, but you have seen pitches like that before, and so you call them. Several of the HRD financial forecasting tasks require you to "call them as you see them" and to move on. Estimating the time to reach a goal is one of those tasks. The pressure you feel comes from the fact that your estimate must have credibility with the decision makers who will review your information.

If a program will be designed by someone else in the HRD department or by an outside provider, have that person make the time estimate. If there are too many political agendas in the work environment, have the manager make it. As in baseball, the official closest to the play calls it. The estimated time to reach the performance goal should be determined for each HRD program option under consideration and recorded in answer to item *e* of the worksheet (Exhibit 1).

Evaluation Period

The evaluation period for our financial forecast is the longest time of all the HRD program options being considered. Thus, the longest of the times entered as item *e* on the worksheet is the proper response to item *f* (Exhibit 1)*:

(*f*) What is the evaluation period?
(Enter the longest time [e] of all the options being considered.)

Getting this number is easy, but it is important to think about the reason for using the *longest time* is the evaluation period. You have already been introduced to the idea that times to reach the work performance goal will vary (see Figure 1). An HRD program option that brings people to the desired performance goal more rapidly should get credit for that performance.

Unstructured HRD situations in which people develop slowly and at relatively low levels of performance must be valued on the same basis as other program options. If they are not, some decision makers will be inclined to wave their "we don't spend money on HRD" flags without ever realizing how much their unstructured HRD programs are actually costing their organization.

*There are instances when longer time-frames are needed to assess results because of organizational norms or data collection restrictions.

Participation

Item *g* of the worksheet (Figure 2), asks:

> (g) How many workers/work groups will participate
> in the HRD program?

The number of participants is usually easy to establish and should already be known from the performance needs assessment. However, the number derived during the needs assessment may not always be in synchronization with the chosen unit of work performance. For example, the total number of sales representatives may be ninety, but the unit of performance may be recorded by sales region, not by the number of individuals in the specified region. If this is the case and there are five sales regions, five is the number of participating *work groups*. In contrast, if the unit of work performance is dollars of sales per individual salesperson, the number of participants would be ninety.

The number of participants is recorded on line *g* of the worksheet (Exhibit 1).

Work Performance During the HRD Program

The calculations for forecasting the performance value of an HRD program, items *h* through *m*, are fairly straightforward and mechanical. With the exception of item *h*, all the calculations use the data you have already entered in the upper portion of the Performance Value Worksheet. Item *h* addresses the issue of work performance *during* the HRD program:

> (h) Will worker/work group produce usable units during the
> HRD program?
> If no, enter -0-
> If yes, enter known performance rate or calculate average
> performance rate $[(b + c)/2]$

Imagine that four new executives are hired by a Fortune 500 firm. The executives are sent with twenty others to a prestigious university for an intensive three-month development program that has been especially designed for the firm. The four new executives do not engage in any work of value to the firm during this period.

A rival firm across town also hires four new executives. The second firm provides just one week of orientation, analyzes the expertise of each of the new executives, negotiates specific work goals with the new executives in their areas of expertise, and provides in-house executive development programs using top executives and local professors who conduct theory-to-practice sessions during the first month that the new executives are employed. The new executives clearly add value to the firm during their development program. Their performance levels during the HRD program can be plotted as rising stairsteps.

We witnessed a simple model of performance-during-development years ago in an organization that provided apprentice-ship training. There we saw trainees learning hand-tool skills and directing their efforts toward producing small parts, most of which in the future would be made by machine in the factory. The purpose of the program was to provide an incentive for learning and to challenge the trainees to match the standards of machine-made products. As limited as the quantity of their production was, the parts they produced during training were salable. They had value.

The main question here is whether or not valued work performance units will be accomplished during the development program. If the answer is yes, the rate and timing of that perform-ance during the HRD program must be determined. Short-term programs that pull people off the job and away from the work site usually yield zero units of performance during the HRD program.

There are two approaches to accounting for situations that combine development and work performance:

- Enter the known performance rate.
- Calculate the average performance rate.

The first approach, entering the known performance rate, acknowledges the fact that HRD programs may conclude with work performances at less-than-goal levels. This is often true where further on-the-job practice will lead to performance at the expected rate. Some HRD options will yield a known number of units of performance at the end of the development period. In this case, enter the known performance numbers on line h of Exhibit 1. To help you visualize various patterns of work performance in structured and unstructured HRD programs, we have shown several plausible options in graphic form (Figure 4).

The second approach allows the forecaster to enter the average performance rate for the HRD options. Studies have shown that where employees are developed on-the-job in an unstructured manner, they produce at a rate of 50 percent or less during the development period (Cullen, Sisson, Sawzin, and Swanson, 1976). Again, this is a conservative estimate. Most practitioners believe that the actual rate is lower than this. Even so, if employees work at the 50 percent level for even short periods of time, this becomes a very expensive method of developing human resources.

For example, let's say a salesperson is expected to manage twelve accounts. Company records show that it has taken, on average, sixteen months for new salespeople to get to this level of performance when they are left to an unstructured HRD program of on-the-job self-development. Organizational performance records may be specific enough for you to calculate the average of actual performance rates for sixteen months. If not, using the average performance rate method $[(b + c)/2]$ yields an average performance of six accounts for new salespeople over the sixteen-month period $[(12 + 0)/2 = 6]$.

In summary, the performance rate during the development period is entered on line h of the worksheet. If no performance is expected, the number entered should be zero. If there is performance and the rate is known, that number should be entered. If there is performance and the rate is not known, it should be estimated at the 50 percent performance level over the development period.

Total Performance During the HRD Program

Item i of the Performance Value Worksheet (Exhibit 1) asks that all work performance during the HRD program for each worker or work group be accounted for.

Figure 4. Variations on Performance During HRD Programs.

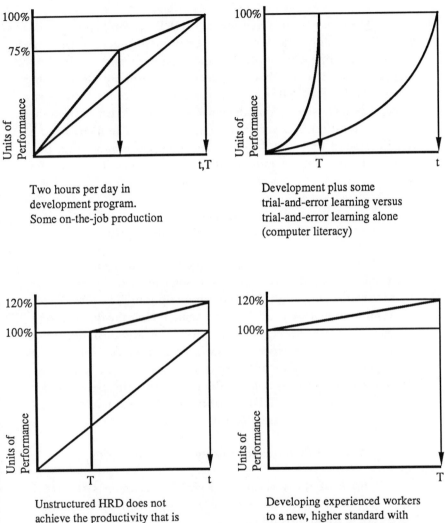

Two hours per day in
development program.
Some on-the-job production

Development plus some
trial-and-error learning versus
trial-and-error learning alone
(computer literacy)

Unstructured HRD does not
achieve the productivity that is
possible with structured HRD

Developing experienced workers
to a new, higher standard with
production during HRD program

100% = current designated standard of performance
T = time to standard performance given structured HRD
t = time to standard performance given unstructured HRD

(*i*) What total units per worker/work group will be produced
during the development time? (*h* × *e*)

Question *i* is answered for each HRD option being considered. With the formula (*h* × *e*), the rate of performance during the
development time is multiplied by the amount of time (in development) required to reach the expected performance level. The
product of this multiplication is entered on line *i* of the worksheet.

The next question on the worksheet, item *j*, differs from the
previous question in a very important manner. The focus is on a
fixed period of time and the estimated *total* performance over that
period of time for the individual or work group. The question
reads:

(*j*) How many units will be produced per worker/work group
during the evaluation period? (*i* + [(*f* – *e*) × *b*])

This fixed evaluation period, the longest of all the development times among the HRD options being considered, provides the
basis for comparing all the HRD program options. The formula for
j determines how many units of time remain after the development
period to the end of the evaluation period (*f* – *e*) and then multiplies
this number times the expected full work performance level (*b*). The
total time of working at full performance *after* completion of the
HRD program [(*f* – *e*) × *b*] is then added to the performance
achieved *during* the HRD program (*i*). The sum is the total
performance in units during the full *evaluation* period.

Value of Performance During Evaluation Period

Item *k* of the worksheet (Exhibit 1) converts the total
expected performance units to be accomplished by individual
workers or work groups into dollars:

(*k*) What will be the value of the worker's/work group's
performance during the evaluation period? (*j* × *d*)

The answer is obtained simply by multiplying the number
of units, line *j*, times the dollar value of a single unit, line *d*. The

result is the total dollar value of the worker or work group's performance during the evaluation period.

Performance Value Gain per Worker/Work Group

The gain in performance is the remaining calculation. The idea is to make sure not to take credit for any work performance achieved before the HRD program is put into place. Item l of the worksheet (Exhibit 1) pursues the performance value gain per worker or work group:

(l) What is the performance value gain per worker/work group?
$$[k - (c \times d \times f)]$$

The formula for l is dominated by c, the performance at the beginning of the HRD program. When it is zero, the formula plays itself out as "k - zero," which equals k. If the beginning performance is greater than zero, the formula acknowledges this beginning performance level and does not allow the HRD program to accept unearned credit for it.

Total Performance Value Gain

At last we come to the item in which the HRD manager is most keenly interested. Item m tells us to compute the performance value gain for all workers/work groups as a result of the HRD program:

(m) What is the total performance value gain for all workers/work groups? ($l \times g$)

Once again, the calculation is a simple one. The performance value per worker or work group (l) is multiplied by the number of workers or work groups (g).

The source of many of the items on the Performance Value Worksheet can be illustrated graphically. The performance-time graph (Figure 3) illustrates for comparison two HRD program options. The first is the longer, unstructured HRD option. The second is the shorter, structured HRD option. Both options show production during the development time. This is one common pattern of development and production. The case that follows illustrates a slightly different pattern in a simplified case. All the information we need to fill out the Performance Value Worksheet is contained in the following description.

Tram Case

You are the training coordinator for the city zoo. The zoo's board of directors would like to make better use of the zoo's valuable volunteers by having them lead tram tours on weekends. The board wants ten trained volunteers, each of whom would lead two one-hour tram tours per weekend. The net income from each tour is $40. No volunteers have previously been entrusted with this job, and you must now decide between two HRD program options. Would it be economically more beneficial to the zoo to train the volunteers by having them learn about the tram tours from experienced staff, or would it be more beneficial to have them study a job aid?

The first option, riding along with experienced operators, will require four hours of training spread over two weekends for each volunteer. The volunteers will perform no tours on their own during the two-week training period. The second option involves assembling job aids that consist of a map, a script, and a manual, which each of the volunteers would study for two hours as their first weekend commitment to the job. The volunteers who participate in this HRD program will perform two tours on their own during the second week. We assume that at the end of either program, each participating volunteer will be fully trained and able to conduct tram tours on his or her own.

Performance Value Worksheet

From the description above, it is clear that a completed tram tour is the appropriate unit of work performance and that the HRD program options are Ride-Along and Job-Aid. Exhibit 2 is a completed Performance Value Worksheet. The performance goal, which can be extracted from the narrative, is two tours per week.

This information is entered as item *b* on the worksheet. All volunteers begin the program with zero performance. None have been exposed to the tram-tour job before this occasion.

The $40 of value per completed tram tour was determined by the zoo's financial manager, who keeps records of income from various zoo operations. Differences in performance between the two options appear on the worksheet where we show that Ride-Along volunteers will take two weeks to reach the performance goal and the Job-Aid volunteers only one week. A total of ten volunteers will participate in this HRD program.

Neither program option results in work performance during the development period (item *h*). Note that a skilled person is operating the tram as the volunteer rides along. Every tram ride during the Ride-Along program is credited to the skilled operator. There is no added value in having the volunteer along, and, in this situation (unlike most other HRD situations) there is no reduction in the performance of the skilled operator.

The unstructured Ride-Along option has a two-week development period during which no volunteers conduct tram tours. The Job-Aid option has a one-week development period during which no volunteers conduct tram tours. This performance information is placed on line *i*. Item *j* asks for the longest development period, two weeks, and lists the units of work performance during that time for both options. In this case, the Job-Aid volunteers conduct two tours during the evaluation period. The Ride-Along volunteers conduct zero tours during the evaluation period.

Items *k* and *l* value the tours at $40 each. Two tours per volunteer, times ten volunteers, or $800, is the total performance value gain for the Job-Aid program. There is zero performance gain for the Ride-Along program during the two-week development period.

It then becomes quite easy to calculate the relative benefits of the two options:

	Ride-Along	*Job-Aid*
Performance Value	$ 0	$800
– Cost	0	$300
Benefit	0	$500

Exhibit 2. Performance Value Worksheet.

Note that performance units and time units for all options must remain consistent throughout the forecast.

Program _Tram Tours_   **Analyst** _C. Bishop_   **Date** _6/2/88_

Option name	1 _Ride-Along_	2 _Job-Aid_
Data required for calculations:		
(a) What **unit** of work performance are you measuring?	_Tour_ unit name	_Tour_ unit name
(b) What is the performance **goal** per worker/work group at the **end** of the HRD program?	2 _Tours_ / _Wk._ no. units / time	2 _Tours_ / _Wk._ no. units / time
(c) What is the performance per worker/work group at the **beginning** of the HRD program?	0 _Tours_ / _Wk._ no. units / time	0 _Tours_ / _Wk._ no. units / time
(d) What **dollar value** is assigned to each performance unit?	$ 40 / unit	$ 40 / unit
(e) What is the **development time** required to reach the expected performance level?	2 _Wks._ no. time	1 _Wk._ no. time
(f) What is the **evaluation period**? (Enter the longest time (_e_) of all options being considered.)	2 _Wks._ no. time	2 _Wks._ no. time
(g) How many workers/work groups will **participate** in the HRD program?	10 no. (workers/groups)	10 no. (workers/groups)

Calculations to determine net performance value:

	Option 1		Option 2	
	0 no.	Tours units	0 no.	Tours units
(h) Will worker/work group produce **usable units** during the HRD program? If no, enter -0-. If yes, enter known performance rate or calculate average performance rate. [(b + c)/2]	0		0	
(i) What total units per worker/work group will be produced during the **development time**? (h x e)		0 no. of units		0 no. of units
(j) How many units will be produced per worker/work group during the **evaluation period**? {[(f – e) x b] + i}		0 no. of units		2 no. of units
(k) What will be the value of the worker's/work group's performance during the evaluation period? (j x d)	$ 0		$ 80	
(l) What is the **performance value gain** per worker/work group? [k – (c x d x f)]	$ 0		$ 80	
(m) What is the **total performance value gain** for all workers/work groups? (l x g)	$ 0 (Option 1)		$ 800 (Option 2)	

We can see that in a two-week period the performance gain from the structured Job-Aid development program outstrips the no-cost unstructured Ride-Along method. Please note, however, that this case involves very short-range thinking—two weeks. If the zoo is open fifty weeks of the year and if the volunteers conduct twenty tours per weekend at $40 each, the net performance value for the year for *each option* would be close to $40,000. The only bad decision in this case would be not to develop the volunteers.

Summary

We offer the following practical tips to help you as you begin to forecast the financial benefits of an HRD program:

- Work with a partner. Having someone to "talk through" forecasts will provide support and reassurance.
- Use a pencil with a big eraser and have extra Performance Value Worksheets at hand.
- Have a calculator handy.
- Record all information in the order in which you receive it. Don't let the order of the items on the worksheet get in your way.
- Beginning forecasters find it easier to work all the way through one HRD option forecast at a time.
- It is important to work with knowledgeable experts to obtain and verify your numbers. Make phone calls or get up from your desk and seek out those individuals who can supply the information you need.
- When in doubt, use the finest scale that is readily available. For example, use hours instead of days and calculate dollars in tens rather than in hundreds. Your numbers can be rounded off later.

Determining performance value is the most complex part of the forecasting process. Additional help follows in the form of five cases presented in the following chapter. Several components are provided for each case, including: (1) the situation, (2) the performance value analysis, and (3) a critique. These five cases will also appear after the costs and benefits chapters that follow.

4

++

Case Examples
of Performance Value Analysis

In this chapter we present five case situations and five completed
Performance Value Worksheets for you to examine in detail. Our
purpose in choosing to include cases from a variety of contexts is
twofold. First, we want you to be aware that the financial benefit
forecasting method can be used in a wide variety of situations—in
the government and private sectors, in manufacturing and service
organizations. It can be used in any situation where HRD programs
contribute to the achievement of valued organizational goals.
Second, we seek to increase your confidence that the method will
work. Through a variety of case examples we demonstrate that the
Performance Value Worksheet can be used to forecast the performance value of HRD programs ranging from organizational development to machine operator training.

In this chapter, we concentrate on introducing the cases and
their respective Performance Value Worksheets. In Chapter Six, we
introduce the Cost Analysis Worksheets for the same cases. In
Chapter Eight, we use the cases to explore the Benefit Analysis
Worksheets and to describe the method and criteria for choosing
among alternative options with the goal of presenting the recommended program option to decision makers. For each case in this
chapter we present a detailed description of the facts of the case, the
completed Performance Value Worksheet for the case, and a critique
of the facts. The cases appear in the following order:

Case 1: Manufacturing. Here, the forecasting method is used
to help in choosing among several HRD options aimed at training production workers who turn out circuit boards (see Exhibits
3 and 4).

Case 2: Service Industry. Learning to use computers to conduct market analyses in the real estate business is the performance goal. For this case, we develop the performance values for three different HRD options (see Exhibits 5 and 6).

Case 3: Organization Development. Achieving a new level of customer service throughout the whole health care organization is the crucial aim of HRD in this case. The ultimate goal is to attract and maintain valued members (see Exhibit 7).

Case 4: Management. A management consulting firm works out its own methods for managing projects. The forecast performance value of a structured HRD program is instructive to decision makers (see Exhibit 8).

Case 5: Public Sector. This case illustrates use of the method in a government setting. The HRD program goal is to develop coaching skills in experienced staff so that the new staff can more rapidly reach skilled performance in the field (see Exhibit 9).

We encourage you to examine the following cases closely. It is important that you be able to see where in the case each piece of data for the Performance Value Worksheet came from and to follow the logic of the calculations through to the total performance value gain.

Although we have limited our discussion of the cases in this chapter to the performance value component of the financial forecasting model, we encourage you to read forward through each of the other two case chapters to gain an overview of the financial benefit forecasting method.

Case 1: Manufacturing

Situation. Profit margins of a manufacturing company that makes specialized circuit boards had been declining. The top management team encouraged departments to participate in a companywide performance needs assessment. The major finding was that inspection rejected far too many of the circuit boards. All the production workers were trained through the unstructured on-the-job training method. It was furthermore discovered that this training method required forty days before a worker could produce three good boards every two days. On the average, the workers read at the fifth-grade level, and they experienced difficulty with the English language.

In addition, ten new production workers were to be hired and would need circuit board training. The options facing management were to continue with the current unstructured training, to develop and deliver an in-house structured training program, or to contract with an experienced consulting training firm that promised to get the workers up to the performance goal in eight days. No circuit boards would be produced during either of the structured training options.

If the structured in-house option were selected, the training staff would team up with the chief electronic engineer to carry out the project. They estimated that in-house structured training would allow workers to reach the performance goal in ten days. Temporary clerical help would be hired to assist during the analysis, design, and development stages. The following additional information will help in analyzing this case:

1. Dollar value per board $600
2. Number of trainees   10
3. Performance goal   1½ circuit boards per day
4. External consultant rate $2,220 per trainee

Critique. This is a straightforward case. The performance needs assessment clearly established a need that could be met by an HRD circuit board training program. Each unit of work performance—a circuit board—is obviously attributable to an individual worker. It is also very likely that production records are kept so that the number of days it takes new circuit board assembly workers to train themselves on the job is known. In this case it took forty days.

The production of usable units during Option 1 (unstructured training) was estimated by using the average rate formula. It is possible that available company records could have instead provided exact rates.

Since assembling the circuit boards is quite labor intensive, the analyst expected that the company had a precise dollar value for each. It did. Just a few unproduced $600 circuit boards or a few boards going into the trash can add up to significant numbers. Both

Exhibit 3. Performance Value Worksheet.

Note that performance units and time units for all options must remain consistent throughout the forecast.

Program _Circuit Boards_ **Analyst** _B. Lawther_ **Date** _5/8/88_

Option name	1 Unstructured	2 In-House
Data required for calculations:		
(a) What **unit** of work performance are you measuring?	Boards (Bds.) unit name	Boards (Bds.) unit name
(b) What is the performance goal per worker/work group at the **end** of the HRD program?	1.5 Bds. / Day no. units / time	1.5 Bds. / Day no. units / time
(c) What is the performance per worker/work group at the **beginning** of the HRD program?	0 Bds. / Day no. units / time	0 Bds. / Day no. units / time
(d) What **dollar value** is assigned to each performance unit?	$ 600 / unit	$ 600 / unit
(e) What is the **development time** required to reach the expected performance level?	40 Days no. time	10 Days no. time
(f) What is the **evaluation period**? (Enter the longest time (e) of all options being considered.)	40 Days no. time	40 Days no. time
(g) How many workers/work groups will **participate** in the HRD program?	10 no. workers/groups	10 no. workers/groups

Calculations to determine net performance value:

	Option 1		Option 2	
(h) Will worker/work group produce **usable units** during the HRD program? If no, enter -0-. If yes, enter known performance rate or calculate average performance rate. [(b + c)/2]	.75 no.	Bds. units	0 no.	Bds. units
(i) What total units per worker/work group will be produced during the **development time**? (h x e)	30 no. of units		0 no. of units	
(j) How many units will be produced per worker/work group during the evaluation period? {[(f − e) x b] + i}	30 no. of units		45 no. of units	
(k) What will be the value of the worker's/work group's performance during the evaluation period? (j x d)	$ 18,000		$ 27,000	
(l) What is the performance value gain per worker/work group? [k − (c x d x f)]	$ 18,000		$ 27,000	
(m) What is the **total performance value gain** for all workers/work groups? (l x g)	$ 180,000		$ 270,000	

Exhibit 4. Performance Value Worksheet.

Note that performance units and time units for all options must remain consistent throughout the forecast.

| Program | Circuit Boards | Analyst | B. Lawther | Date | 5/8/88 |

Option name	3	Consultant	4

Data required for calculations:

(a) What unit of work performance are you measuring?

      Boards (Bds.)
         unit name   unit name

(b) What is the performance goal per worker/work group at the **end** of the HRD program?

    1.5   Bds. / Day   _____ / _____
    no.   units / time   no.   units / time

(c) What is the performance per worker/work group at the **beginning** of the HRD program?

    0   Bds. / Day   _____ / _____
    no.   units / time   no.   units / time

(d) What **dollar value** is assigned to each performance unit?

    $ 600   / unit $ _____ / unit

(e) What is the **development time** required to reach the expected performance level?

    8   Days   _____ _____
    no.   time   no.   time

(f) What is the **evaluation period**? (Enter the longest time (e) of all options being considered.)

    40   Days   _____ _____
    no.   time   no.   time

(g) How many workers/work groups will participate in the HRD program?

    10   _____
    no. workers/groups   no. workers/groups

Calculations to determine net performance value:

		Bds.		
	0	*units*	*0*	*units*
	no.		no.	
(h) Will worker/work group produce **usable units** during the HRD program? If no, enter -0-. If yes, enter known performance rate or calculate average performance rate. [(b + c)/2]				
(i) What total units per worker/work group will be produced during the **development time**? (h x e)	*0* no. of units		no. of units	
(j) How many units will be produced per worker/work group during the **evaluation period**? {[(f − e) x b] + i}	*48* no. of units		no. of units	
(k) What will be the value of the worker's/work group's performance during the **evaluation period**? (j x d)	$ *28,800*		$	
(l) What is the **performance value gain** per worker/work group? [k − (c x d x f)]	$ *28,800*		$	
(m) What is the **total performance value gain** for all workers/work groups? (l x g)	$ *288,000* (Option 3)		$ (Option 4)	

of the structured training programs promised to get the workers producing at the performance goal in relatively short periods of time—eight and ten days versus forty days. Therefore, over the entire evaluation period either of these two options would yield about $10,000 additional performance value per worker. Multiply this times ten workers, and the total net performance difference for the structured training options was about $100,000 more than for the unstructured option.

Case 2. Service Industry

Situation. The service organization you work for provides real estate market analyses for brokers. Business is expanding and you, the HRD director, have been asked to look closely at the people-performance issues related to executing market analyses and initiating a new hiring campaign.

Each analysis takes an hour to perform when it is executed by a competent analyst using a personal computer connected to a mainframe computer. There is a $70 fee for each analysis. Your company is about to hire twenty-five new analysts. Until now, new analysts were trained through an unstructured on-the-job method that required six weeks before the analyst was "up to speed." A "buddy" spent about twenty hours with a new analyst during this period.

The vendors who sold you the software program and trained the first ten analysts want to contract with you for additional development services. They could deliver training at their facility (105 miles away) over a three-day period. Their charge would include two consultants for each day of training and twenty days of development time.

For an in-house option you estimate seven full days (fifty-six hours) of training, with trainees being unable to produce usable market analyses during the development period. Experience has shown that it takes your department two hours of non-HRD expert time for each hour of structured training attributable to the project. Trainee and HRD staff time does not need to be covered.

Costs available from company records include:

Salaries:	Participants	$24,000 to $28,000
	Administrative support	$16,000 to $20,000

HRD professionals	$23,000 to $25,000
Subject matter experts	$26,000 to $32,000
Miscellaneous support personnel	$16,000 to $20,000

Fringe and overhead: 38 percent rate

Travel: 26 cents per mile; $40 per diem; $80 per night

Facilities: $75 per day for a minimum of twenty people off site
$50 per day for a maximum of 30 people on site

Maintenance: $50 per day on site

Equipment: PC purchase $4,000; PC rental $500 per week

Materials: consumables $500; reusable $700

Outside services: fees $80 per hour; travel mileage plus hourly; direct costs estimated at 20 percent of fee

Critique. This company, which started small, formally oriented and trained its original employees in the company values and work methods. In subsequent years, however, orientation training for new hires has relaxed into an unstructured "buddy" system. A new spurt of growth has management again thinking about providing structured training for its market analysts.

While management is committed to structured training, the HRD staff felt it important to analyze the existing unstructured conditions so as to retain perspective. The two structured options vary. One is three days long, the other is seven days long. One is on site, the other is off site. One yields usable products during training, the other does not. Even with the differences, this analysis is fairly straightforward. The unit of performance [market analysis] is clear and easily attributable to individual employees. The worth of that unit is known by the company.

While the inefficiency of the existing unstructured development program is shocking, this is typical of fast-growing companies that do not take the time to analyze what is happening in the midst of their success.

Case 3. Organization Development

Situation. Universal Healthcare operates in a very aggressive market. The organization's market researcher has pointed out that

Exhibit 5. Performance Value Worksheet.

Note that performance units and time units for all options <u>must remain consistent</u> throughout the forecast.

Program _Market Analysis_ **Analyst** _L. Swenson_ **Date** _4/30/88_

Option name	1 _Unstructured_	2 _Vendor_
Data required for calculations:		
(a) What unit of work performance are you measuring?	_Market Analysis (M.A.)_ unit name	_Market Analysis (M.A.)_ unit name
(b) What is the performance goal per worker/work group at the end of the HRD program?	$\dfrac{1}{\text{no.}}$ $\dfrac{M.A.}{\text{units}}$ / $\dfrac{Hr.}{\text{time}}$	$\dfrac{1}{\text{no.}}$ $\dfrac{M.A.}{\text{units}}$ / $\dfrac{Hr.}{\text{time}}$
(c) What is the performance per worker/work group at the **beginning** of the HRD program?	$\dfrac{0}{\text{no.}}$ $\dfrac{M.A.}{\text{units}}$ / $\dfrac{Hr.}{\text{time}}$	$\dfrac{0}{\text{no.}}$ $\dfrac{M.A.}{\text{units}}$ / $\dfrac{Hr.}{\text{time}}$
(d) What **dollar value** is assigned to each performance unit?	\$ _70_ / unit	\$ _70_ / unit
(e) What is the **development time** required to reach the expected performance level?	$\dfrac{240}{\text{no.}}$ $\dfrac{Hr.}{\text{time}}$	$\dfrac{24}{\text{no.}}$ $\dfrac{Hr.}{\text{time}}$
(f) What is the **evaluation period**? (Enter the longest time (e) of all options being considered.)	$\dfrac{240}{\text{no.}}$ $\dfrac{Hr.}{\text{time}}$	$\dfrac{240}{\text{no.}}$ $\dfrac{Hr.}{\text{time}}$
(g) How many workers/work groups will **participate** in the HRD program?	$\dfrac{25}{\text{no. workers/groups}}$	$\dfrac{25}{\text{no. workers/groups}}$

Calculations to determine net performance value:

	(Option 1)	(Option 1)	(Option 2)	(Option 2)
	.5	M.A.	0	M.A.
	no.	units	no.	units
(h) Will worker/work group produce **usable units** during the HRD program? If no, enter –0–. If yes, enter known performance rate or calculate average performance rate. [(b + c)/2]				
(i) What total units per worker/work group will be produced during the **development time**? (h x e)	120 no. of units		0 no. of units	
(j) How many units will be produced per worker/work group during the **evaluation period**? {[(f – e) x b] + i}	120 no. of units		216 no. of units	
(k) What will be the value of the worker's/work group's performance during the **evaluation period**? (j x a)	$ 8,400		$ 15,120	
(l) What is the **performance value gain** per worker/work group? [k – (c x d x f)]	$ 8,400		$ 15,120	
(m) What is the **total performance value gain** for all workers/work groups? (l x g)	$ 210,000		$ 378,000	

Exhibit 6. Performance Value Worksheet.

Note that performance units and time units for all options <u>must remain consistent</u> throughout the forecast.

Program _Market Analysis_   **Analyst** _L. Swenson_   **Date** _4/30/88_

	Option name	3 In-House	4
Data required for calculations:			
(a) What **unit** of work performance are you measuring?		*Market Analysis (M.A.)* ‾‾‾‾‾‾‾‾‾‾ unit name	‾‾‾‾‾‾‾‾‾‾ unit name
(b) What is the performance goal per worker/work group at the **end** of the HRD program?		*1* / *M.A.* / *Hr.* no. / units / time	/ no. / units / time
(c) What is the performance per worker/work group at the **beginning** of the HRD program?		*0* / *M.A.* / *Hr.* no. / units / time	/ no. / units / time
(d) What **dollar value** is assigned to each performance unit?		$ *70* / unit	$ / unit
(e) What is the **development time** required to reach the expected performance level?*		*56* / *Hr.* no. / time	/ no. / time
(f) What is the **evaluation period**? (Enter the longest time (e) of all options being considered.)		*240* / *Hr.* no. / time	/ no. / time
(g) How many workers/work groups will **participate** in the HRD program?		*25* no. (workers)/groups	‾‾‾‾‾‾‾‾‾‾ no. workers/groups

Calculations to determine net performance value:

	0 ___ M.A. ___ units no.	0 ___ ___ units no.
(h) Will worker/work group produce usable units during the HRD program? If no, enter -0-. If yes, enter known performance rate or calculate average performance rate. [(b + c)/2]		
(i) What total units per worker/work group will be produced during the development time? (h x e)	0 no. of units	no. of units
(j) How many units will be produced per worker/work group during the evaluation period? {[(f − e) x b] + i}	184 no. of units	no. of units
(k) What will be the value of the worker's/work group's performance during the evaluation period? (j x d)	$ 12,880	$
(l) What is the performance value gain per worker/work group? [k − (c x d x f)]	$ 12,880	$
(m) What is the total performance value gain for all workers/work groups? (l x g)	$ 322,000 (Option 3)	$ ___ (Option 4)

Exhibit 7. Performance Value Worksheet.

Note that performance units and time units for all options <u>must remain consistent</u> throughout the forecast.

Program __Customer Service__ Analyst __B. Webb__ Date __3/15/88__

Option name	1 In-House	2 Consultant
Data required for calculations:		
(a) What unit of work performance are you measuring?	Members (Mbr.) unit name	Members (Mbr.) unit name
(b) What is the performance goal per worker/work group at the **end** of the HRD program?	$\dfrac{1400}{\text{no.}}$ $\dfrac{Mbr.}{\text{units}}$ / $\dfrac{Yr.}{\text{time}}$	$\dfrac{500}{\text{no.}}$ $\dfrac{Mbr.}{\text{units}}$ / $\dfrac{Yr.}{\text{time}}$
(c) What is the performance per worker/work group at the **beginning** of the HRD program?	$\dfrac{0}{\text{no.}}$ $\dfrac{Mbr.}{\text{units}}$ / $\dfrac{Yr.}{\text{time}}$	$\dfrac{0}{\text{no.}}$ $\dfrac{Mbr.}{\text{units}}$ / $\dfrac{Yr.}{\text{time}}$
(d) What **dollar value** is assigned to each performance unit?	$ $\dfrac{200}{\quad}$ / unit	$ $\dfrac{200}{\quad}$ / unit
(e) What is the **development time** required to reach the expected performance level?	$\dfrac{1}{\text{no.}}$ $\dfrac{Yr.}{\text{time}}$	$\dfrac{1}{\text{no.}}$ $\dfrac{Yr.}{\text{time}}$
(f) What is the **evaluation period**? (Enter the longest time (e) of all options being considered.)	$\dfrac{1}{\text{no.}}$ $\dfrac{Yr.}{\text{time}}$	$\dfrac{1}{\text{no.}}$ $\dfrac{Yr.}{\text{time}}$
(g) How many workers/work groups will **participate** in the HRD program?	$\dfrac{1}{\text{no. workers/groups}}$	$\dfrac{1}{\text{no. workers/groups}}$

Calculations to determine net performance value:

		Option 1			Option 2	
	no.		Mbr. units	no.		Mbr. units
(h) Will worker/work group produce **usable units** during the HRD program? If no, enter -0-. If yes, enter known performance rate or calculate average performance rate. [(b + c)/2]	700			250		
(i) What total units per worker/work group will be produced during the **development time**? (h x e)		700 no. of units			250 no. of units	
(j) How many units will be produced per worker/work group during the **evaluation period**? {[(f − e) x b] + i}		700 no. of units			250 no. of units	
(k) What will be the value of the worker's/work group's performance during the **evaluation period**? (j x d)	$ 140,000			$ 50,000		
(l) What is the **performance value gain** per worker/work group? [k − (c x d x f)]	$ 140,000			$ 50,000		
(m) What is the **total performance value gain** for all workers/work groups? (l x g)	$ 140,000 (Option 1)			$ 50,000 (Option 2)		

its services are not much different from those of its competitors. She further has stated that there is room for growth in the company's market. As director of HRD you agree with top management's conviction that poor customer service is a serious problem for Universal Healthcare and that an organization development program aimed at creating a new "sense of the customer" in all employees will result in maintaining current members and attracting new members. Plans include a companywide organization development effort to instill a "sense of the customer" in all of Universal's employees and a specific customer relations training program for ten salespeople whose goal is to attract new members.

The options are to produce an in-house organization development program using Universal's HRD staff or to use a similar off-the-shelf program that is available from an external development firm. Both programs will involve participants in several sessions over the next year. The in-house version promises a gain of 1,400 members in one year's time. The gain from the off-the-shelf program is expected to be 500 in the same time period. Healthcare's financial director estimates that one new member, after all expenses, leaves Universal Healthcare with $200 net profit. The in-house program is expected to cost $24,000, the off-the-shelf program $15,000.

Critique. This case has four very interesting aspects. First, the unit of work performance—new members—was easy to identify and very difficult to value. Only a few people at the top of the organization knew the dollar value of the annual net profit from each membership. It took quite a bit of probing to finally discover it.

Second, since all employees of the organization participated in the customer-service program, the entire organization was considered to be a single work group. The increase in membership was not an individual worker goal—it was an organizational goal.

Third, the custom-made in-house program, because of its goodness of fit to the problem, promised to be much more effective in terms of expected performance at the end of the one-year evaluation period (1,400 members) than the generic off-the-shelf version (500 members). An extension of this issue had to do with the accounting procedures used by Universal Healthcare. A membership sale is based on a business calendar year. Thus, a new member joining at midyear only pays and joins for half a year. This unit is thus a one-half member rather than a full member. Because of this, and because the exact performance rate was not known, the average membership units for the two options during the evaluation period were calculated. They were 700 for the in-house program and 250 for the generic version.

Fourth, there was no comparison made to existing conditions. The organization had gone beyond looking at that option and was clearly in the mood to act. The question under consideration was which of the two structured HRD programs to choose.

Case 4: Management

Situation. A division of a large management consulting firm specializes in the design and installation of information systems for business clients. The systems include computers, computer software, and system know-how. The firm has developed a well-publicized systems approach to which their consultants closely adhere when working with client projects. The system has five major phases and three dozen specific steps.

Four project directors supervise ten to twelve consultants, seeing to it that the original contracts are honored and that the "system" of the firm is followed. A performance needs assessment revealed that project directors were experiencing uneven work flow, stalled projects, and projects of uneven quality, which had the long-term potential of affecting the market position of their firm. Simply stated, many of the information system projects were out of control.

The HRD department worked with the four project directors to propose a new project management work system to increase the efficiency and quality of projects. The new work system was to provide an efficient means for monitoring, planning, and communicating the design and installation of information systems. The executive vice-president of operations and the comptroller determined that strict adherence to the quality features of the firm's "system" and potential gains in efficiency would result in a first-year market share gain of 1 percent, worth $150,000 in net profit.

Exhibit 8. Performance Value Worksheet.

Note that performance units and time units for all options must remain consistent throughout the forecast.

Program _Project Management_   **Analyst** _C.A.S._   **Date** _7/1/88_

Option name	1 Unstructured	2 Project Mgt.
Data required for calculations:		
(a) What unit of work performance are you measuring?	_Percent Market Share (M.S.)_ unit name	_Percent Market Share (M.S.)_ unit name
(b) What is the performance goal per worker/work group at the end of the HRD program?	$\dfrac{41}{\text{no.}}$ $\dfrac{M.S.}{\text{units}}$ / $\dfrac{Yr.}{\text{time}}$	$\dfrac{42}{\text{no.}}$ $\dfrac{M.S.}{\text{units}}$ / $\dfrac{Yr.}{\text{time}}$
(c) What is the performance per worker/work group at the beginning of the HRD program?	$\dfrac{41}{\text{no.}}$ $\dfrac{M.S.}{\text{units}}$ / $\dfrac{Yr.}{\text{time}}$	$\dfrac{41}{\text{no.}}$ $\dfrac{M.S.}{\text{units}}$ / $\dfrac{Yr.}{\text{time}}$
(d) What **dollar value** is assigned to each performance unit?	$ $\underline{\ 150,000\ }$ /unit	$ $\underline{\ 150,000\ }$ /unit
(e) What is the **development time** required to reach the expected performance level?	$\dfrac{1}{\text{no.}}$ $\dfrac{Yr.}{\text{time}}$	$\dfrac{1}{\text{no.}}$ $\dfrac{Yr.}{\text{time}}$
(f) What is the **evaluation period**? (Enter the longest time (_e_) of all options being considered.)	$\dfrac{1}{\text{no.}}$ $\dfrac{Yr.}{\text{time}}$	$\dfrac{1}{\text{no.}}$ $\dfrac{Yr.}{\text{time}}$
(g) How many workers/work groups will participate in the HRD program?	$\dfrac{1}{\text{no. workers/groups}}$	$\dfrac{1}{\text{no. workers/groups}}$

Calculations to determine net performance value:

	41	M.S.	42	M.S.
(h) Will worker/work group produce usable units during the HRD program? If no, enter -0-. If yes, enter known performance rate or calculate average performance rate. [(b + c)/2]	no. ___	units ___	no. ___	units ___
(i) What total units per worker/work group will be produced during the **development time**? (h x e)	41 ___ no. of units		42 ___ no. of units	
(j) How many units will be produced per worker/work group during the **evaluation period**? {[(f − e) x b] + i}	41 ___ no. of units		42 ___ no. of units	
(k) What will be the value of the worker's/work group's performance during the **evaluation period**? (j x d)	$ ___ 6,150,000		$ ___ 6,300,000	
(l) What is the **performance value gain** per worker/work group? [k − (c x d x f)]	$ ___ 0		$ ___ 150,000	
(m) What is the **total performance value gain** for all workers/work groups? (l x g)	$ ___ 0 (Option 1)		$ ___ 150,000 (Option 2)	

Critique. This is an interesting case for several reasons. First, the mere existence of a logical information system does not mean that it is known who does what and when. A seemingly logical system can get out of control or may never have really been under control. In this case, the information system was never really under control. Even so, the firm has 41 percent of the market share to show for its information system and good personnel. What is now needed is a good *project management system* to orchestrate the client needs, the information system, the consultants, and the project directors.

Second, without the new project management system, the firm's performance was forecast to remain steady. With a new work method in place, a modest 1 percent increase in market share is forecast by the end of the first year.

A third interesting point is the selection of market share percentage as the unit of work performance. The original performance needs assessment focused on day-to-day inefficiencies and the slipping quality features of the information system. This information was instrumental in designing the new project management system but was set aside in favor of percent of market share gain when the decision about unit of performance was made. This is a difficult but logical leap. Also, the worth of market share gains was estimated by top executives in the firm.

Case 5: Public Sector

Situation. The HRD manager of a public-sector auditing and collection agency regularly put groups of new recruits through a 240-hour training course before sending them off to work in the field. The course was, however, just the beginning of their training. On average, an additional fifteen months were required for the new staff to become competent. Believing that the time to reach full performance could be shortened, the training manager gathered a committee of eight experts to discuss the situation and to devise a plan for accelerating learning on the job. Their strategy was a simple one: teach the experienced staff how to be more effective coaches of the new staff. After exploring several alternative packages for teaching coaching skills, the committee settled on the option of asking the National Association of Auditors to conduct a four-day training program. This option was then compared to the current, more leisurely method of gaining full competency. Ten experienced staff who generally coached one new worker each would be trained. The committee asked the training manager to conduct a forecast cost-benefit analysis of the project and to include the committee's work in the project's costs. Establishing the unit of performance as dollars of collections per hour and a performance standard of $175 of collections per hour required a consensus decision on the part of several top managers.

Critique. Forecasting the net performance value in this case presents an obstacle worth noting. The unit of performance was rather arbitrarily determined. An auditor-collector works with a number of clients who have extremely diverse characteristics. Thus one client's work could take many days to process while another's could be processed in a few hours. Clients' personalities and the variety of their economic endeavors confound the issue of finding an appropriate unit of performance. The professional status of the auditor-collector also created problems in identifying a measurable unit of work performance. Finally, however, dollars collected was established as the primary performance unit for purposes of the forecast. Past records of exemplary, average, and below-average performers provided the basis for setting an average of $175 in identified collections per hour as the primary performance goal of the development program. This average figure accommodated all the types and sizes of clients that any one auditor-collector could be expected to work with over a period of time.

Clearly, one could be genuinely concerned that the unit of performance set for purposes of the forecast not be carried into the trainee's workplace as the single measure of quality work performance. The measure does have great utility in forecasting, but it may also distort performance in the workplace over time. Finding a single simple measure of performance for a previously undefined job has the potential of intoxicating managers with ideas of "control." Such quantity-only goals could end up encouraging dishonesty, and the leveraging of "profitable" clients, and result in generally poor customer service in the workplace.

Exhibit 9. Performance Value Worksheet.

Note that performance units and time units for all options must remain consistent throughout the forecast.

Program _Coaching Skills_ **Analyst** _C. Sleezer_ **Date** _3/1/88_

Option name	1 _Unstructured_	2 _NAA Course_
Data required for calculations:		
(a) What unit of work performance are you measuring?	_Dollar ($)_ unit name	_Dollar ($)_ unit name
(b) What is the performance goal per worker/work group at the **end** of the HRD program?	$\dfrac{175}{\text{no.}}$ $\dfrac{\$}{\text{units}} / \dfrac{Hr.}{\text{time}}$	$\dfrac{175}{\text{no.}}$ $\dfrac{\$}{\text{units}} / \dfrac{Hr.}{\text{time}}$
(c) What is the performance per worker/work group at the **beginning** of the HRD program?	$\dfrac{0}{\text{no.}}$ $\dfrac{\$}{\text{units}} / \dfrac{Hr.}{\text{time}}$	$\dfrac{0}{\text{no.}}$ $\dfrac{\$}{\text{units}} / \dfrac{Hr.}{\text{time}}$
(d) What **dollar** value is assigned to each performance unit?	$\quad 1 \quad$ / unit	$\quad 1 \quad$ / unit
(e) What is the **development time** required to reach the expected performance level?	$\dfrac{2625}{\text{no.}}$ $\dfrac{Hrs.}{\text{time}}$	$\dfrac{2250}{\text{no.}}$ $\dfrac{Hrs.}{\text{time}}$
(f) What is the **evaluation period**? (Enter the longest time (e) of all options being considered.)	$\dfrac{2625}{\text{no.}}$ $\dfrac{Hrs.}{\text{time}}$	$\dfrac{2625}{\text{no.}}$ $\dfrac{Hrs.}{\text{time}}$
(g) How many workers/work groups will participate in the HRD program?	$\dfrac{10}{\text{no. workers/groups}}$	$\dfrac{10}{\text{no. workers/groups}}$

Calculations to determine net performance value:

	87	$	87	$
	no.	units	no.	units
(h) Will worker/work group produce **usable units** during the HRD program? If no, enter -0-. If yes, enter known performance rate or calculate average performance rate. [(b + c)/2]				
(i) What total units per worker/work group will be produced during the **development time**? (h x e)	228,375		195,750	
	no. of units		no. of units	
(j) How many units will be produced per worker/work group during the **evaluation period**? {[(f − e) x b] + i}	228,375		261,375	
	no. of units		no. of units	
(k) What will be the value of the worker's/work group's performance during the **evaluation period**? (j x d)	$ ___ 228,375		$ ___ 261,375	
(l) What is the **performance value gain** per worker/work group? [k − (c x d x f)]	$ ___ 228,375		$ ___ 261,375	
(m) What is the **total performance value gain** for all workers/work groups? (l x g)	$ ___ 2,283,750		$ ___ 2,613,750	
	(Option 1)		(Option 2)	

5

+++

Forecasting Costs
of HRD Programs

Most serious discussions about the economics of human resource development (HRD) begin with costs. This is unfortunate. To forecasters and decision makers who understand performance values, costs become less important than the expected economic benefits of HRD.

"How much will it cost?" "What will we have to spend on that program?" In many organizations, managers view the HRD department as nothing more than a financial burden. To them, HRD is a drain on earnings, not an investment in the future capability of the organization. Through the use of performance value analyses, however, HRD programs can be seen as enhancing the capability of the organization. In this chapter, we present a worksheet to aid the forecaster in estimating and forecasting HRD costs. The purpose of the worksheet is to gather all the cost information needed to calculate the cost portion of the financial forecasting model.

Credibility is Essential

Current practices include a variety of methods for assigning the costs of HRD programs. In some organizations the HRD department is designated a cost center, while in others it is designated a profit center. Sometimes HRD is buried in the personnel department, and some organizations do not assign any costs at all to HRD programs at the corporate level.

HRD as a Cost Center. A cost center is a point in the accounting records at which costs associated with a department are collected. All expenditures that are connected with a cost center are collected, recorded by category, and presented for review. When HRD is designated as a cost center, the HRD manager tends to concentrate on keeping the costs of essential HRD programs as low as possible. A major concern is how to implement programs in less expensive ways. Thus, when HRD is a cost center, efficiency can become more important than effectiveness. For example, orientation programs tend to shrink until they are two hours long, and new employees are left to learn the values and mores of the organization by other means. Usually, line management picks up at least some of the costs of HRD programs. Extended meetings, telephone time, downtime on production machinery, and salaries paid while supervisors attend organization development programs are allocated under various line items in operations. When line managers are not convinced of the value of HRD, they may claim an inability to find the funds to pay for proposed HRD programs unless "corporate will pay for it." When this happens, HRD dollars shrink still more.

HRD as a Profit Center. Some HRD departments have been assigned profit responsibilities. The HRD staff primarily works to develop programs that address the needs of the parent organization. In addition to this activity, staff members are expected to add to the profitability of the company by marketing these same programs to other organizations. The Acme HRD department, for example, becomes Acme HRD Systems with its own product development, marketing, and sales functions—and corporate expectations for profitable operations.

HRD as a Support Service to Operations. More often, especially in smaller organizations, HRD programs compete with recruiting, benefits management, and records management for resources. The costs of HRD programs are charged back to the department that requested them, or they are buried in a variety of personnel accounts.

In all these circumstances, the true costs of specific HRD programs can be difficult to determine. But this is history. We are discussing forecasting, which has a future focus. For forecasting purposes, thorough cost analyses are needed. No matter how the costs of past HRD programs have been recorded, HRD professionals are challenged to use their analytical skills in gathering cost data for use in forecasting the costs of a proposed HRD program. Fortunately, once you understand the challenge, you, like most HRD managers, will have little trouble deciding how to forecast and where to assign program costs.

Presenting Proposals to Management

Few would deny that HRD programs are costly. The most visible costs are incurred during the implementation phase of an HRD program. Implementation expenses such as travel, meals, meeting rooms, and facilitators add up quickly. These expenses grow even larger as more and more people become involved in the program. But implementation costs represent only part of the total costs of HRD programs. Every phase of every program—analysis, design, development, implementation, and evaluation—brings its costs. In Chapter Three we walked through a worksheet to use in forecasting the performance value for a proposed program. In this chapter, we will walk through a worksheet to use in analyzing program costs. The Cost Analysis Worksheet can be customized to fit any HRD program or system. In the benefit-forecasting model, total program costs are subtracted from the performance value to yield the expected economic benefit to the organization. How precisely to handle these costs when presenting a proposal for an HRD program to management depends on the expectations of management. Needless to say, the confidence that comes from knowing the benefits expected to result from an HRD activity permits a certain integrity in analyzing and forecasting the direct and indirect costs to be incurred by that activity.

Analyzing Costs

In comparison to the challenge of calculating the perform-ance value of an HRD program, the task of forecasting program costs seems relatively straightforward. But as is usually the case in such matters, nothing is as simple as it first appears. For example, how would you answer the following questions:

1. Should overhead, or burden, be included in program costs?
2. What are all the real costs of an HRD program?
3. Are all the costs included in your proposal?

The answer to the first two questions is: *It all depends.* If your company customarily charges a certain cost item to HRD or to another department, you will propose charging the cost the same way. For instance, all copy expenses may be charged to administration, regardless of which department incurred them. This distinction is explained later in the chapter. The answer to the third question is: *You ought to have a good estimate of the costs of their programs,* but the costs that you include in your proposals to management depend on the custom of your company and on your situation. When you forecast costs, we urge you to observe two principles:

- Don't leave out any major cost items.
- Don't include unnecessary or exaggerated cost items.

Violating the first principle can ruin the integrity of your forecast and destroy your credibility in an instant. One astute challenge from management about a missing cost item can raise suspicions that your forecast may not be a trustworthy foundation on which to base an important development decision. Violating the second principle can lead to overestimating costs and can mean the difference between acceptance and rejection of your proposal.

Systematic analysis is the key to finding and forecasting all the essential cost items to be included in an HRD proposal. But before we discuss the costs that will be incurred by HRD programs, we must review the language of costs.

What Is a Cost?

Of the several definitions of *cost* in *Webster's Third New International Dictionary,* two are of particular interest:

- "An item of outlay incurred in the operation of a business enterprise (as for the purchase of raw materials, labor, services, supplies) including depreciation and amortization of capital assets"
- "Whatever must be given, sacrificed, suffered, or forgone to secure a benefit or accomplish a result"

Sacrifice may be too strong a word, but the second definition does describe the subjective feelings that decision makers often experience when they think about supporting and paying for HRD programs. A major premise of this book is that HRD professionals can begin to communicate with decision makers more clearly about the expected performance values of HRD. We believe you can maximize the possibility that decision makers in your company will objectively review the true costs and benefits of a proposed HRD program option.

But the first definition of a cost—"an item of outlay that is *incurred in the operation of [HRD programs]*"—seems to fit our purposes better. From this definition arises the necessity for constructing a cost picture of each proposed HRD option. But when was the last time you talked about or even thought about amortizing a capital asset, that is, spreading its costs over time? Maybe never. While *amortization* may not be part of your daily vocabulary, you should remain open to the possible necessity of calculating such items as direct and indirect costs, fixed and variable costs, and amortization. The goal is to present *accurate* and *appropriate* HRD proposals to decision makers. Fortunately, you don't have to do all the figuring yourself. Help is usually either a visit or a phone call away. An example will clarify the difference between simple and elaborate cost analysis.

In response to an identified performance need, two internal HRD consultants proposed team-building programs for twenty-five managers of the Mentax Company. The first consultant was the picture of thoroughness: "I figure we'll need four meeting rooms in the Lake Building. Now let's see . . . the building is six years old and is expected to remain usable for twenty-four more years. It cost $1.3 million. Taxes are $7,000 per year, maintenance is $4,300 per year. And landscaping, which is expected to last ten years, cost

$5,500. The four rooms come to about one-sixteenth of the building. So, dividing $1.3 million by thirty and adding $7,000 for taxes, $4,300 for maintenance, and $550 for landscaping will give the annual cost. Now I divide the thirty hours we expect to use the rooms by 2,000 hours and I get . . ."

The second consultant used more expedient methods: "I figure we'll need four meeting rooms in the Lake Building. I called the person who schedules the meeting rooms. He said we could figure on being charged $300 a day for the use of all four rooms, or $200 for every morning that we have scheduled. So, ten morning meetings comes to $2,000 for facilities."

We recommend that, whenever possible, you use the second approach to calculating HRD costs. Even though it is simple, it is *accurate* and *appropriate*. As a busy HRD professional you have many important tasks to do. Making elaborate calculations about the use of facilities is the job of the facilities manager, who probably has the figures already prepared. Furthermore, figures supplied by the facilities manager or the comptroller will likely carry more credibility than will the carefully and painstakingly calculated figures of the HRD manager.

Using Financial Terminology

When talking with decision makers, it is a good idea to use either standard financial terminology or the same terminology that they use. Your effectiveness in communicating your HRD proposals increases greatly when you learn to use cost terminology that will be understood by the decision makers in your company.

What Is an HRD Cost? An HRD cost is any expenditure that the organization chooses to attribute to an HRD program. If the organization does not normally associate a particular cost—such as the cost of facilities, office supplies, or telephones—with an HRD program, even though that cost might legitimately be charged to HRD, it *does not* have to be included in a forecast of costs of the program. What is an HRD cost in one organization may not necessarily be considered an HRD cost in another. Some costs are fixed no matter how many programs the HRD department runs.

Some costs vary. Some costs can be directly attributed to specific HRD programs. Some cannot. We describe these and other cost terms and categories next.

Fixed Costs. These are costs that are incurred no matter how many programs the HRD department produces. HRD staff salaries, office rent, utilities, and insurance are fixed costs. Two video decks, one in the conference room and one that travels from division to division with a set of videotapes on using performance appraisal techniques, may represent either a fixed cost of the HRD department or a variable cost directly attributable to a program. Employing a secretary at a salary of $20,000 plus 25 percent fringe benefits incurs a fixed cost of $25,000 to the HRD department. If the HRD department erects a facility in which to conduct its programs, its fixed costs could rise dramatically. A thorough analysis of HRD costs will identify a base-line set of fixed costs that will not vary directly with the number of programs or the number of participants.

Variable Costs. These costs generally increase or decrease with the number of programs run or participants involved. Each additional program entails costs, such as travel to conduct a needs assessment. The fewer the number of programs, the lower these costs. Variable costs increase as participation in HRD programs increases. Each additional participant incurs a package of costs that may include, for example, the cost of handouts, manuals, coffee, lunches, travel, and lodging. The greater the number of participants, the greater the variable costs.

Direct Costs. These are expenditures that are directly attributable to a specific program. Such costs would not exist if the program did not exist. For example, typewritten materials, printed brochures, and the labor of the outside vendor who produces them are direct costs to the program with which they are associated. Such costs are usually charged to the individual HRD program that incurs them.

Indirect Costs. These costs are associated with keeping the HRD department operating. They may be fixed costs or they may rise and fall with the level of activity in the department. Indirect costs are expenditures that are not directly attributable to a specific program. Hiring a second secretary, repainting a classroom, and renting a copy machine are indirect costs that are not fixed costs. They are also not chargeable to a specific program. Indirect costs tend to be invisible to the users of HRD programs. The HRD manager's salary, office supplies for the HRD department, and the monthly telephone bill are indirect costs. Slide and overhead projectors that are used or made available for *all* programs are indirect costs. Some program costs, such as outlays for paper and pencils, may be considered indirect because the amount of these materials used for any one program is too small to justify the expense of allocating them to individual programs. Sometimes HRD is charged with proportional costs for expensive items such as audiovisual equipment or furnishings. These indirect costs are too large to be paid for by individual programs. Such costs are written off over a period of ten or more years through regular charges to the department. They appear as a line item on yearly or monthly budgets.

Indirect costs of HRD may be charged to the corporate administration or personnel budgets, or they may be charged proportionately to all the HRD programs for the year. For instance, in some organizations, travel is put into a general travel account. In other organizations, travel is itemized according to who is traveling to what destination for what reason. In these organizations, travel for HRD and travel for sales would be recorded differently.

Charge-Backs and Overhead. The profit-making functions in organizations must eventually pay for HRD programs. In other words, HRD programs are a cost that burdens manufacturing or other line activities. Operations pay for HRD through charge-backs and through overhead. When a program is designed for and delivered to operations, the receiving department may agree to pick up the bill for travel, meals, and lodging for all participants. In addition, it may agree to be charged for facilitator fees, participant materials, and other program-specific costs. These costs are "charged back" to the receiving department. The receiving department may or may not be expected to pay for the costs of the needs assessment, the organization and job analysis, or the use of meeting rooms. Such expenditures could be charged to profit-generating operations through overhead.

Is HRD ever required to pay for company overhead? Sometimes. We have heard of an HRD department that was charged for the executive copy machine. Sadly, members of the department didn't get to see their fancy copy machine in person, let alone use it.

Marginal Costs and Step Costs. These terms are not commonly used, but they are important to keep in mind when delivering a proposal to management. A marginal cost is the change in outlay that occurs when one more participant is added to the program roster. Sometimes, however, no marginal cost occurs when more participants are added. For example, if a management consultant will speak to seventy executives for $5,000, the marginal cost for the seventy-first and seventy-second executives in attendance will probably be zero. The speaker will charge no more for two extra people. Thus the forecaster can often assume some flexibility in costs when adding a few more participants to a particular HRD activity.

Step costs rise incrementally. The cost of a team-building program will remain constant when ten to twenty people will be involved. But if we add a twenty-first person, it may be necessary to find a larger room and run another printing of handouts. The larger room and the additional run of handouts will take care of thirty people. But if we add a thirty-first person, we may again have to make other arrangements. And so on through stairstep changes in costs. As you develop your forecasts, keep in mind the flexibilities and rigidities of cost patterns.

Our listing of cost terms is by no means complete, but it will suffice to alert you to the need to understand and use managerial language when forecasting the costs of proposed programs. For the appropriate cost terminology in your particular organization, you might look to written material such as other successful proposals, departmental budgets, financial statements, and monthly productivity reports. In addition, you could interview other department heads who have successfully presented proposals to management.

What cost terminology did they use? Please note that the essence of wisdom is to ask knowledgeable others to review your proposal before taking it to a meeting of decision makers.

There are no right or wrong ways to talk about costs. You are trying to make sure that your cost items are consistent with the customary cost categories in your company. You will want to include the cost items that the decision makers in your company are sure to be concerned about. You must decide whether to include a portion of HRD annual fixed (indirect) costs in your proposal or whether to exclude such costs because they would be considered irrelevant to the proposed program. For example, if administration generally lends its meeting rooms for your programs, meeting room costs will not appear on your forecast Cost Analysis Worksheet.

Cost Analysis Worksheet

HRD can be viewed as a system as well as a program. Direct costs arise during every phase of the systematic processes that HRD professionals employ. The general process behind HRD programs consists of five phases:

1. Analysis
2. Design
3. Development
4. Implementation
5. Evaluation

These are our terms for each of the phases. You may describe your systematic HRD practices with other terms. For accurate forecasts, the expenses that will be associated with each HRD program phase must be estimated and totaled. Most programs will involve several phases. Purchased programs are the exception to this rule because the design and development phases are lumped into the purchase price of the package or into the fee charged by the external consultant. Even so, customizing a standard HRD program to meet the specific needs of your company will incur costs. Such costs will be assigned to the development phase. The basic Cost Analysis Worksheet (Exhibit 10) is a useful guide for analyzing when and where most direct costs will be incurred by a proposed HRD program.

High-quality human resource development comes about only in the process of meeting critical organizational needs. For this reason, identifying a specific performance need is one goal of the first phase of the HRD process. For example, the HRD manager travels to a subsidiary to interview several people about a problem they have identified. Once there, the manager finds that the data-input people are making numerous mistakes in categorizing certain types of information. The analyst discovers that there are two reasons for these errors. First, the clerks lack an understanding of how the data will be used. Second, the system that they are working with is unusually complex. The analyst interviews several supervisors of the data-input clerks, too. They verify the need for redesigning (simplifying) at least a part of the work system and for special training for the part of the job that cannot be redesigned. Needs assessment activities are part of the analysis phase.

Analysis Phase. Managers often recognize and voice the need for an HRD program to deal with a particular problem in the organization—perhaps noticeable friction among top managers or a lawsuit over sexual harassment may highlight the need for an HRD program. Typically, you or your consultant will personally investigate the problem before beginning to design a solution.

During this analysis phase, staff costs will be incurred whenever you use observations, interviews, or surveys, or whenever you gather and review organizational records for purposes of collecting and recording base-line data. A thorough needs assessment can require quite a commitment of staff time. In a large organization, interviewing the people who are concerned with the problem or opportunity could take several days and involve extensive travel. Expenses for materials during the analysis phase will be large if you intend to conduct a formal survey. Postage and sundry expenditures will be anticipated. Sometimes copies of organizational records will be gathered. On occasion, you will hire an external consultant to conduct a more sophisticated or more objective needs analysis than the capabilities of the internal staff will allow. The consultant's fee is entered as a cost of the analysis

Exhibit 10. Cost Analysis Worksheet.

Program _____ Analyst _____ Date _____

Option name	1 _____	2 _____
Analysis:		
Needs assessment	_____	_____
Work analysis	_____	_____
Proposal to management	_____	_____
Other _____	_____	_____
Other _____	_____	_____
Design:		
General HRD program design	_____	_____
Specific HRD program design	_____	_____
Other _____	_____	_____
Other _____	_____	_____
Development:		
Draft and prototype	_____	_____
Pilot test and revise	_____	_____
Production and duplication	_____	_____
Other _____	_____	_____
Other _____	_____	_____
Implement:		
Program management	_____	_____
Program delivery	_____	_____
Participant costs	_____	_____
Other _____	_____	_____
Other _____	_____	_____
Evaluation:		
Program evaluation and report	_____	_____
Performance follow-up	_____	_____
Other _____	_____	_____
Other _____	_____	_____
Total HRD program costs	$ _____	$ _____
	(Option 1)	(Option 2)

phase, as are his or her travel and lodging expenses and any support services anticipated. The major result of this analysis phase is a proposal for both HRD and management actions to address a specific performance need. Some secretarial help may be needed to prepare the proposal for presentation to management.

Sometimes, when the HRD need is for technical skills training—for example, when new machinery or new work systems are anticipated—extensive analyses of work behavior will be required. Job descriptions and task analyses must be recorded, procedures must be documented, and process and troubleshooting analyses must be developed. Be aware that analysis of work behavior can be a time-consuming task.

Perhaps an analysis of a subject area is indicated. For example, a review of the literature on performance appraisal may be planned. New, well-researched appraisal methods will be used to evaluate the appraisal system currently in use in your company. Examining the performance appraisal process in the work setting and conducting a literature search take a lot of time. But careful analytical work yields much useful material for inclusion in a performance management program. Miscellaneous cost items in the analysis phase will include secretarial service for typing the analysis worksheets and research assistance for gathering library materials.

Design Phase. The primary task of the design phase is planning the details of the HRD program. Because this work primarily requires the expertise of the HRD professional, few costs other than the cost of the designer's time will be involved. Nevertheless, this cost can be significant. The designer will take into account such variables as the number and characteristics of program participants, the objectives to be achieved, and the process to achieve them. Designing a program, outlining the progression of activities, and working through the details of what people must do to achieve the desired results of the HRD program can involve a lot of careful, detailed thinking. Perhaps an off-the-shelf program will accomplish the same goals. But research to find just the right package or one that can be tailored to the company and to the specific performance need also takes time.

Development Phase. In this phase, the materials that will be used during the HRD program are created, purchased, or located. Such materials include job aids, films, values clarification instruments, and participant packets. If expensive media are forecast for the HRD program, costs could rise dramatically. Creating a video, a slide and tape show, or a job reference manual calls for the use of expensive artistic and writing skills. Creating an interactive video or computer-based instruction program could require up to 200 hours of development time for every one hour of running time. When your department does not have the talent needed to develop the proposed media, you will have to hire artists, instructional designers, and scriptwriters, and you may also have to rent studios. Developing pretests and posttests, as well as pilot testing and revising HRD programs, involves additional costs that you must anticipate for this phase.

Implementation Phase. Here we find ourselves in the more visible portion of the iceberg of HRD costs. Most decision makers recognize the necessity of paying for facilitators and instructors, travel to and from an HRD session, meals and lodging, paper-and-pencil instruments for assessing management styles, and a television monitor for picking up remote programs via satellite. These costs are significant, but the largest HRD costs that will be incurred during the implementation phase are the salaries of participants. Twenty managers attending a strategic planning workshop for a day can ring up quite a bill for their time. But unlike hourly workers who attend HRD programs, managers may be expected to make up the work they miss. No work left undone means no charge for salaries to the HRD program. As a forecaster of costs, you must anticipate making such cost decisions.

Sending executives to M.B.A. programs and machine operators to vestibule training can also lead to costs in the form of tuition, materials, and fees. Career development programs involve costs for tests and counseling. All such costs are forecast under the implementation phase. Given the extensive participant costs incurred during the implementation phase, the staffing costs incurred during this phase can seem quite modest. Thus, the direct costs of staff to deliver an HRD program may appear small. In contrast, the direct cost of materials used may be quite high, especially if the cost of mistakes made on the way to learning important work skills is counted. The costs of books, manuals, handouts, and other consumable items must be estimated, as must the costs of distributing information about the HRD program and meals for participants.

Evaluation Phase. If your program involves a large investment, or if you believe that management will want to look at the HRD record later, the advantages of evaluating your HRD programs will be quite clear. In the press of trying to determine costs for other program phases, however, forecasters sometimes neglect to forecast the costs that will be incurred during the evaluation phase. Following up on the results of HRD programs deserves at least as much attention as do the other program phases. Ideally, three successive levels of evaluation will be pursued to determine the results of an HRD program, and each involves costs.

First, are the participants satisfied with the results of the HRD program? Designing, administering, collecting, and compiling participant satisfaction ratings take staff time. The satisfaction ratings of the supervisors or executives who requested and paid for the HRD effort must also be gathered, compiled, and analyzed.

Second, what new knowledge and behaviors or what new expertise has been gained as a result of the program? Creating, administering, and scoring knowledge and performance tests take staff time. Materials costs could also be incurred as new abilities to understand concepts, manipulate machines, and complete paper work are demonstrated.

Third, what changes in individual, work-group, or organizational performance can be expected to occur as the result of the HRD program? Measures of performance will be gathered and compared with the base-line data to be collected during the needs assessment phase. Staff time will be needed either to make or to follow up on these measurements.

Converting performance measures, and whatever it takes to achieve them, into dollars and cents is the financial benefit level of performance evaluation. Financial benefit *forecasting* is done in the initial HRD program phase—in the proposal step. Financial benefit *analysis* is done in the evaluation phase. During the evaluation phase, the actual performance value and cost and benefit figures are collected, and the Cost Analysis and Performance Value worksheets are again filled out. These actual figures will be compared to the forecast figures. Comparing actual performance values and actual costs and benefits with forecast performance values, costs, and benefits will aid you in improving your forecasting skills.

Total Direct and Indirect Costs. There can be little doubt that HRD programs are costly. The forecast total of direct costs attributable to even a modest in-house program will often be larger than a first, quick estimate indicates. You may wish to use the cost list in the last pages of Chapter Six as a memory jogger whenever you complete the Cost Analysis Worksheet for an HRD program.

Consistency Is Needed

The Performance Value Worksheet (Exhibit 1) and the Cost Analysis Worksheet are used together. One complements the other. The HRD forecaster needs both worksheets to form a true picture of each option. Our experience shows that it is better to complete the Performance Value Worksheet for an option before attempting to forecast the costs for that option. One caution about filling in the cost worksheet is in order, namely, it must be compiled in figures that are consistent with those of the Performance Value Worksheet. When the forecaster fills out one of the two worksheets on the basis of a total program, the other should be filled out on the same basis. Both worksheets can also be filled out per work group or per individual worker. Just be sure to focus on the group or function that will be involved in the HRD activity.

One more area of consistency is important. When determining costs, you may find that the managers in your company do not agree on which items to include on the cost sheet and what dollar costs should be assigned to them. It is important that you use a consistent framework for bounding each option under consideration. Without close attention to this detail, you could end up comparing the proverbial apples and oranges instead of two comparable HRD options.

Depending on the custom in your company, you may want to estimate the total amount of the indirect costs (see previous discussion on cost terminology) of the HRD department and add a portion of these to the program forecast at the bottom of the worksheet.

Summary

In this chapter, we have defined cost terminology as it is used in many organizations. Some HRD costs are easy to uncover but some can be found only after extensive and careful digging. Asking the right people for pertinent cost figures and knowing what HRD costs the decision makers expect to see on your forecasts are important to your success in the role of forecaster. At first glance, completing the Cost Analysis Worksheet appears to be an easier task than completing the Performance Value Worksheet, but don't be fooled. In the next chapter we discuss how to fill out the Cost Analysis Worksheet.

6

++++++++++++++++++++++++++++++++++++++

Case Examples
of Cost Analysis

In this chapter we present cases to help you understand and use the Cost Analysis Worksheet. We have taken the cost figures from the case situations in Chapter Four and entered them in a Cost Analysis Worksheet for each case. The cost figures for the first four cases are simple and straightforward. Some, but not all, of the costs in the Cost Analysis Worksheets found in this chapter were spelled out in the case situations introduced in Chapter Four. The Cost Analysis Worksheets for Case 1: Manufacturing are illustrated in Exhibits 11 and 12. No costs were forecast for the unstructured option. Costs of $17,856 were forecast for the In-House option and $22,200 for the Consultant option. Exhibits 13, 14, 15, and 16 show the Cost Analysis Worksheets for Cases 2, 3, and 4. We will use Case 5: Public Sector to conduct a thorough discussion of the kind of thinking that a forecaster uses when analyzing costs and assigning dollar amounts of costs to the various HRD program phases. (If you want to challenge yourself, stop reading now and try your hand at filling in a blank cost sheet for Case 1. Compare your version with ours. Do not be too concerned if you put some of the cost figures in different places. The important part is not to omit a critical cost.) The Cost Analysis Worksheet for Case 5 is shown in Exhibit 17. Saved for last in this chapter is a discussion of the subject of customizing a cost worksheet to fit your organization.

In-Depth Cost Analysis of Case 5: Public Sector

The HRD manager of a government auditing and collection agency regularly put groups of new recruits through an extensive formal training course before sending them off to work in the field.

Exhibit 11. Cost Analysis Worksheet.

Program ___*Circuit Boards*___ Analyst ___*B. Lawther*___ Date ___*5/8/88*___

	Option name	1 *Unstructured*	2 *In-House*
Analysis:			
Needs assessment			*3,224*
Work analysis			*510*
Proposal to management			
Other _____			
Other _____			
Design:			
General HRD program design			*1,100*
Specific HRD program design			*2,440*
Other _____			
Other _____			
Development:			
Draft and prototype			*1,000*
Pilot test and revise			*600*
Production and duplication			*120*
Other _____			
Other _____			
Implement:			
Program management			*2,294*
Program delivery			*5,760*
Participant costs			
Other _____			
Other _____			
Evaluation:			
Program evaluation and report			*208*
Performance follow-up			*600*
Other _____			
Other _____			
Total HRD program costs		$ *0*	$ *17,856*
		(Option 1)	(Option 2)

Exhibit 12. Cost Analysis Worksheet.

Program   _Circuit Boards_   Analyst   _B. Lawther_   Date _5/8/88_

Option name	3 _Consultant_	4 _____
Analysis:		
Needs assessment		
Work analysis		
Proposal to management		
Other _____		
Other _____		
Design:		
General HRD program design		
Specific HRD program design		
Other _____		
Other _____		
Development:		
Draft and prototype		
Pilot test and revise		
Production and duplication		
Other _____		
Other _____		
Implement:		
Program management		
Program delivery	22,200	
Participant costs		
Other _____		
Other _____		
Evaluation:		
Program evaluation and report		
Performance follow-up		
Other _____		
Other _____		
Total HRD program costs	$ 22,200	$ _____
	(Option 3)	(Option 4)

Exhibit 13. Cost Analysis Worksheet.

Program   _Market Analysis_   Analyst   _L. Swenson_   Date   _4/30/88_

Option name	1 _Unstructured_	2 _Vendor_
Analysis:		
Needs assessment		
Work analysis		
Proposal to management		
Other _____		
Other _____		
Design:		
General HRD program design		6,000
Specific HRD program design		6,800
Other _____		
Other _____		
Development:		
Draft and prototype		
Pilot test and revise		
Production and duplication		
Other _____		
Other _____		
Implement:		
Program management		
Program delivery		12,290
Participant costs		
Other _("Buddy Salaries")_	5,000	
Other _____		
Evaluation:		
Program evaluation and report		200
Performance follow-up		
Other _____		
Other _____		
Total HRD program costs	$ 5,000	$ 25,290
	(Option 1)	(Option 2)

Exhibit 14. Cost Analysis Worksheet.

Program _Market Analysis_ Analyst _L. Swenson_ Date _4/30/88_

Option name	3 _In-House_	4 _____
Analysis:		
Needs assessment		
Work analysis	9,421	
Proposal to management		
Other _____		
Other _____		
Design:		
General HRD program design		
Specific HRD program design	3,000	
Other _____		
Other _____		
Development:		
Draft and prototype	1,000	
Pilot test and revise		
Production and duplication	200	
Other _____		
Other _____		
Implement:		
Program management	300	
Program delivery	580	
Participant costs		
Other _____		
Other _____		
Evaluation:		
Program evaluation and report	200	
Performance follow-up		
Other _____		
Other _____		
Total HRD program costs	$ 14,701	$ _____
	(Option 3)	(Option 4)

Exhibit 15. Cost Analysis Worksheet.

Program _Customer Service_   Analyst _B. Webb_   Date _3/15/88_

Option name	1 _In-House_	2 _Consultant_
Analysis:		
Needs assessment	5,000	
Work analysis	5,000	
Proposal to management	1,000	
Other _____	2,000	
Other _____		
Design:		
General HRD program design	1,500	
Specific HRD program design	2,500	
Other _____		
Other _____		
Development:		
Draft and prototype	500	
Pilot test and revise		
Production and duplication	500	
Other _____		
Other _____		
Implement:		
Program management	2,500	
Program delivery	2,500	15,000
Participant costs		
Other _____		
Other _____		
Evaluation:		
Program evaluation and report	500	
Performance follow-up	500	
Other _____		
Other _____		
Total HRD program costs	$ 24,000	$ 15,000
	(Option 1)	(Option 2)

Exhibit 16. Cost Analysis Worksheet.

Program _____Project Management_____ Analyst ___C.A.S.___ Date __7/1/88__

Option name	1 _Unstructured_	2 _Project Mgt._
Analysis:		
Needs assessment		2,000
Work analysis		2,000
Proposal to management		500
Other _____		
Other _____		
Design:		
General HRD program design		500
Specific HRD program design		1,000
Other _(consultant review)_		1,000
Other _____		
Development:		
Draft and prototype		2,000
Pilot test and revise		4,000
Production and duplication		500
Other _____		
Other _____		
Implement:		
Program management		1,000
Program delivery		5,000
Participant costs		
Other _____		
Other _____		
Evaluation:		
Program evaluation and report		500
Performance follow-up		1,000
Other _____		
Other _____		
Total HRD program costs	$ _____	$ ___21,000___
	(Option 1)	(Option 2)

Exhibit 17. Cost Analysis Worksheet.

Program _Coaching Skills_   Analyst _C. Sleezer_   Date _3/1/88_

	Option name	1 _Unstructured_	2 _NAA Course_
Analysis:			
	Needs assessment		3,296
	Work analysis		
	Proposal to management		70
	Other _(tuition and time)_		680
	Other		
Design:			
	General HRD program design		
	Specific HRD program design		412
	Other		
	Other		
Development:			
	Draft and prototype		
	Pilot test and revise		
	Production and duplication		280
	Other _(HRD manager)_		82
	Other		
Implement:			
	Program management		
	Program delivery		3,000
	Participant costs		38,400
	Other _(HRD manager)_		164
	Other		
Evaluation:			
	Program evaluation and report		989
	Performance follow-up		
	Other _(secretarial)_		42
	Other		
Total HRD program costs		$	$ 47,415
		(Option 1)	(Option 2)

The course was, however, just the beginning of their training. On average, an additional fifteen months, or 2,625 hours, of on-the-job unstructured training was required before the new staff reached the performance standard of $175 worth of collections per hour. Believing that the time needed to reach full performance could be shortened, the HRD manager established a committee of eight internal experts to discuss the situation and to devise a plan for accelerating learning on the job. The strategy they recommended was a simple one: teach the experienced staff how to be more effective coaches of the new staff. After exploring several alternative packages for teaching coaching skills, the committee settled on the option of asking the National Association of Auditors (NAA) to conduct a four-day coaching skills program for the ten experienced field people who would be coaching the trainees. With this option, the new staff could be expected to reach the performance standard in thirteen months, or 2,250 hours. The committee asked the HRD manager to forecast the benefit expected for the coaching skills program and compare it with the current, more leisurely on-the-job method of helping trainees reach full competency. Further, the committee insisted that the cost of its own work be included in the program cost forecast.

The Cost Analysis Worksheet for the coaching skills program is shown in Exhibit 17. The HRD manager has forecast the costs of the program to the nearest dollar as follows:

Analysis. The expenses of the committee would primarily fall within this phase. A check of wage classifications and rates showed that, on average, each committee member's salary amounted to $15 per hour. With benefits added, the cost of each member's time was calculated to be about $20.60 per hour. The committee planned to meet about five times for four hours each time. Committee time for the project would total $3,296.00 ($20.60 per hour × 4 hours × 5 meetings × 8 members). No food or travel costs for committee members would be charged to the program.

Two of the committee members planned to prepare for the work of the committee by meeting with a class at a local college to study effective coaching. Eight hours of class time and a tuition fee of $175.00 for each totaled about $680.00 [($20.60 per hour × 8 hours × 2 members) + ($175.00 tuition fee × 2 members)].

Writing the HRD proposal to the director of the agency was to be done in committee sessions, but typing the proposal would require the skills of a secretary. Secretarial time was valued at $10.60 per hour including benefits. Five hours would be needed to type, duplicate, and distribute the proposal to management. Total secretarial and duplication costs were forecast to be about $70.00 [($10.60 per hour × 5 hours) + $17.00 duplication cost].

Design. The major expense of this phase would be incurred in changing some of the language of the presenter's script and the case studies and altering other small procedural details of the NAA's usual coaching skills program. Two people working about ten hours would be needed to customize the program, and this would cost $412.00 ($20.60 per hour × 10 hours × 2 staff).

Development. The major expense for this phase would be for typing and duplicating a customized coaching manual for each of the twelve participants at a cost of $20 per manual. The forecast total for this phase is $280 [($20 per manual × 10 coaches) + 4 extra].

About four hours of the HRD manager's time would be needed to telephone each of the ten participants to prepare them to attend the session. The telephone time would be used to discuss any concerns that the manager-coaches might have. This time was forecast to cost about $82.00 ($20.60 per hour × 4 hours).

Implementation. The HRD manager planned to spend one-half day briefing the ten coaches before turning them over to the NAA trainer. This half day would be followed by three days of customized training. After the training, the HRD manager again planned to spend one-half day with the participating coaches—this time in a debriefing session. (The cost of the coaches' lost productivity for four days and the HRD manager's time for one day would be included in the cost forecast. The NAA trainer's time would be included in the fee to be paid to the NAA for the entire course.) The HRD manager's time for one day of meeting with the coaches was expected to cost about $164.00 ($20.60 per hour × 8 hours).

The HRD manager believed that the coaches' productivity would drop about 50 percent during the four days of training. The drop was not forecast at $240 per hour (full rate) because the coaches would presumably have projects in motion and problems with these projects could be handled by a phone call or two as needed during the four days they would be off the job. One of the committee members who was planning to attend the training as a coach verified this presumption. The lost productivity would amount to $38,400 ($120 per hour × 8 hours × 4 days × 10 coaches).

A call to the NAA established that the fee to be paid to it as compensation for the use of one trainer for three days and for the original course content would be roughly $1,000 per day, for a total of $3,000.

No travel or food expenses were expected or forecast.

Evaluation. The HRD manager believed that two government evaluators would spend three days in monitoring the training, evaluating the results, and reporting to the agency director. Their time for evaluation and reporting would amount to just under $989.00 ($20.60 per hour × 8 hours × 3 days × 2 trainers).

Typing, duplicating, and distributing the evaluation report were expected to take three hours of secretarial time, or about $32.00 ($10.60 per hour × 3 hours). Duplicating the report was expected to cost another $10.

Cost Analysis Decisions. Perhaps not perfectly obvious are two decisions that were made to ensure that costs were not unnecessarily overstated. The first decision was not to estimate the cost of the meeting room where the program would be delivered. It is the site for all regular meetings of the collection staff, and no differentiation is made among the variety of activities held there. The second, and more crucial, decision was to charge to the program 50 percent of the coaches' lost productivity during their time in the program. The coaches' salaries while in training were easily covered by the 50 percent of their productivity not charged to the program. Charging for time lost *and* productivity lost would have overstated the cost of the program.

How Much Do HRD Programs Cost?

We can't spell out the specific costs of your HRD programs. For one thing, many items are more expensive in certain regions of the country than they are in others. In addition, some organizations prefer to go first-class all the way, while others prefer business or even economy class. We offer just one rule: *When in doubt about the cost of any item, ask.* Don't create cost estimates out of blue sky. Check your records of past programs, or better yet, pick up the phone and call the conference center to ask about the prices of lunches for 100 people. A travel agent will be pleased to provide the prices of airline tickets from far-flung divisions to headquarters. The compensation and benefits expert in your company can inform you about the salary ranges of prospective participants. The plant manager will tell you that overhead is charged at a rate of 80 percent to 100 percent of direct labor costs. If you get your numbers from the experts in your company, they will find little in your forecast to argue with later.

The media expert at the local college knows the prices you will have to pay for so many minutes of film, audiotape, or video. That same expert is qualified to tell you how much it costs to have a slide produced and that videodisk costs are far too high for most applications. Sometimes you can find talented artists and photographers among fellow employees in your company. Free-lancers, whom you can find through your local professional associations, will be pleased to quote their ballpark figures for writing a 200-page job manual. Consultants are generally willing to discuss the price of their services. Some fast legwork and a couple of hours of telephoning will yield an amazing number of accurate cost estimates.

Customizing the Cost Analysis Worksheet

Every organization is unique. Decision makers in various organizations will attend to very different cost items. In one organization, managers will expect an accounting for every hour of every employee who is even peripherally involved in an HRD program. In another organization, managers will pay close attention to the costs of such items as facilities used and materials printed and then assume that staff time is a given for which no accounting need be made. In some organizations every travel voucher must be properly assigned to a particular HRD program. In other organizations, however, managers allow HRD programs a generous travel budget and ask for little in the way of accounting. This last type of financial management is potentially troublesome because sooner or later the HRD manager will have to answer questions about the costs of HRD programs. Without any reporting requirements, the HRD forecaster will have a problem deciding what costs to account for.

In any case, most proposals to decision makers will be based on a customized Cost Analysis Worksheet especially tailored to fit your organization. There are many ways to categorize cost items for your cost forecasts. We sometimes use a *People* and *Things* classification system to help us remember to include important HRD cost items in our forecasts.

In the *People* category, your job is to estimate their times at their rates of pay, including a percentage for benefits:

- Analysts—needs analysts, job analysts, system analysts, other researchers
- Developers—artists, instructional designers, creative writers, computer programmers, subject matter experts, photographers
- Facilitators—instructors and trainers, group facilitators, consultants
- Support personnel—typists, secretaries, messengers, chauffeurs, researchers
- Participants—trainees, clients, recruits

In the *Things* category, your job is to gather data on quantities and prices:

- Equipment—production machinery, copiers, computers, typewriters, recorders, videocassette recorders, television sets, overhead projectors, cameras, simulators
- Facilities—tables and chairs, flip charts, rental fees
- Supplies—paper, markers, newsprint, transparencies

- Services—transportation, literature search fees, food, lodging, art and photography, studio rental, telephone

A customized Cost Analysis Worksheet for your company might include the people and things categories and look like the one in Exhibit 18. Most of the major costs of each HRD phase will be incurred under the people category. For instance, conducting needs assessments, completing work analyses, and proposing programs to management are the three activities of the analysis phase that require human work. Under each HRD program phase, you will want to include the salaries and consultant fees of the people who accomplish each of the necessary tasks. Sometimes all the tasks of the analysis and evaluation phases are done by the HRD manager, while other people will be brought in to complete the remaining phases—instructional developers, media specialists, group process consultants. Don't forget to include the salary costs of support personnel and participants. Also included in each HRD phase are the costs of things—equipment, supplies, facilities, and services. If an organization *never* charges for the use of its meeting facilities, the worksheet can be designed without a line for facilities.

Exhibit 19 illustrates the use of a customized cost analysis worksheet for the coaching skills case. The total costs are the same as in Exhibit 17, but individual costs are listed under different descriptors. You must decide which worksheet gives the more useful cost picture. At any rate, the following tips can serve as a guide for the novice forecaster:

- Costs should be figured in a way that is consistent with the Performance Value Worksheet.
- Record your assumptions and the bases for your cost decisions. Follow the example of Case 5 in this chapter and write down the thinking behind the figures on the Cost Analysis Worksheet.
- Forecasting is a big-picture operation. Don't be too concerned with gathering and recording all the small, insignificant costs.
- Remember that your audience may consist of people from various levels in your company. Identify which costs they are interested in and the level of detail they require. The kinds and

types of costs and the level of detail you use should be based on the immediate audience, the secondary audience (others who will review your proposal), and the custom in your company.

- Use realistic cost estimates.
- Don't leave out a cost that you and others consider critical to the success of the program.
- Don't count any cost more than once.
- Sit in on meetings and note how your manager and others present information. Follow their lead when you deliver your proposal. Check with your mentor if you have one.
- If you are projecting costs far into the future, add a fudge factor.
- Start today to keep good records of program costs. In the future you will save time by referring to your records.

For additional help in analyzing costs, we refer you to three useful books. Although each of the authors treats the subject of costs in depth, be aware that their emphasis is on *evaluating* training programs rather than on *forecasting* HRD benefits for purposes of decision making.

In *Training Cost Analysis*, (1985), Glenn E. Head provides a primer on costing. Step-by-step, the author leads the reader through a series of mathematical formulas into which the HRD manager enters current or projected program cost data. In the words of the author, the guide is "simple but comprehensive." Although the model focuses on training, it can be used in analyzing the costs of any HRD program.

Lyle M. Spencer, Jr.'s *Calculating Human Resource Costs and Benefits* (1986) offers a "simple, how-to-do-it guide" for giving "hard" dollar numbers to "soft" human resource projects and programs. The author provides programming instructions in BASIC for setting up a variety of worksheets.

Finally, in *Costs, Benefits, and Productivity in Training Systems,* Greg Kearsley presents statistical analysis of the costs and benefits of ongoing training in large organizations. If your company is large and if statistical graphs are important in forecasting and evaluating your HRD programs, you may wish to consult this work.

Exhibit 18. Customized Cost Analysis Worksheet.

Program _____ Analyst _____ Date _____

Option name	1 _____	2 _____
Analysis:		
People:		
Needs assessment (salaries)	_____	_____
Work analysis (salaries)	_____	_____
Proposal to management (salaries)	_____	_____
Other _____	_____	_____
Things:		
Equipment _____	_____	_____
Supplies _____	_____	_____
Facilities _____	_____	_____
Services _____	_____	_____
Other _____	_____	_____
Design:		
People:		
General program design (salaries)	_____	_____
Specific program design (salaries)	_____	_____
Other _____	_____	_____
Things:		
Equipment _____	_____	_____
Supplies _____	_____	_____
Facilities _____	_____	_____
Services _____	_____	_____
Other _____	_____	_____
Development:		
People:		
Draft and prototype (salaries)	_____	_____
Pilot test and revise (salaries)	_____	_____
Production and duplication (salaries)	_____	_____
Other _____	_____	_____

Things:
    Equipment _____
    Supplies _____
    Facilities _____
    Services _____
    Other _____

Implement:
  People:
    Program management (salaries)
    Program delivery (salaries)
    Participants (salaries)
    Other _____
  Things:
    Equipment _____
    Supplies _____
    Facilities _____
    Services _____
    Other _____

Evaluation:
  People:
    Evaluation and report (salaries)
    Performance follow-up (salaries)
    Other _____
  Things:
    Equipment _____
    Supplies _____
    Facilities _____
    Services _____
    Other _____

Total HRD program costs $ _____ $ _____
                           (Option 1)   (Option 2)

Exhibit 19. Customized Cost Analysis Worksheet.

Program _Coaching Skills_   **Analyst** _C. Sleezer_   **Date** _3/1/88_

	Option name	1 _Unstructured_	2 _NAA Course_
Analysis:			
People:			
Needs assessment (salaries)			2,296
Work analysis (salaries)			1,000
Proposal to management (salaries)			383
Other _____			
Things:			
Equipment _____			
Supplies _____			
Facilities _____			
Services _(committee training fee)_			350
Other _(postage)_			17
Design:			
People:			
General program design (salaries)			100
Specific program design (salaries)			312
Other _____			
Things:			
Equipment _____			
Supplies _____			
Facilities _____			
Services _____			
Other _____			
Development:			
People:			
Draft and prototype (salaries)			53
Pilot test and revise (salaries)			82
Production and duplication (salaries)			20
Other _____			

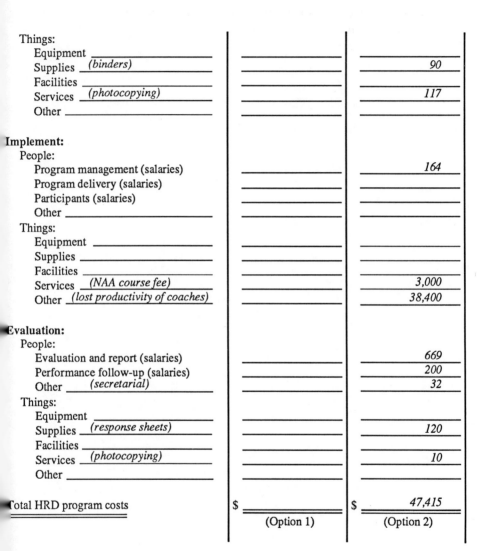

Things:
  Equipment _____
  Supplies _(binders)_ — 90
  Facilities _____
  Services _(photocopying)_ — 117
  Other _____

Implement:
  People:
    Program management (salaries) — 164
    Program delivery (salaries)
    Participants (salaries)
    Other _____
  Things:
    Equipment _____
    Supplies _____
    Facilities _____
    Services _(NAA course fee)_ — 3,000
    Other _(lost productivity of coaches)_ — 38,400

Evaluation:
  People:
    Evaluation and report (salaries) — 669
    Performance follow-up (salaries) — 200
    Other _(secretarial)_ — 32
  Things:
    Equipment _____
    Supplies _(response sheets)_ — 120
    Facilities _____
    Services _(photocopying)_ — 10
    Other _____

Total HRD program costs $ _____ (Option 1) $ 47,415 (Option 2)

There are many books and articles on the subject of postprogram evaluation of the costs and benefits of HRD, but few indeed on the subject of forecasting the financial benefits of HRD programs. The task of translating evaluation language into forecasting language remains for you to do.

7

++

Projecting Financial Benefits
and Presenting Proposals
to Management

This chapter aims to increase your understanding of forecasting financial benefits and to develop your skill in presenting proposals for HRD programs to decision makers in your company. As you will soon see, calculating the benefit of an HRD program is easy. You simply subtract the forecast cost of the HRD program from the forecast performance value. The remainder is the forecast financial benefit. But learning how to present your financial forecast and how to moderate your proposal to accommodate the concerns of decision makers are another matter. Before we look at these aspects of the model, however, it may be worth reviewing Gene Williams's experience with financial forecasting in a service organization.

Two Views of Benefits

Gene Williams is HRD director for a service organization in a fast-moving and highly competitive market. Everybody likes Gene, and he knows it. He is very skilled at using his likable personality to achieve what he thinks is best for his company. As in the case of many HRD professionals, much of Gene's success is related to his ability to listen, to empathize, and to meet the expectations of management. No question about it, Gene has been successful. One indicator of this success is his becoming director of HRD in less than five years. Sometime ago, however, Gene realized that he was not being included in the critical decision-making activities of his company. He felt stymied in his goal to contribute more to company decisions.

A few years back Gene had taken a major step toward this goal by beginning to learn about the economics of human development. After several discussions with a colleague from another firm, Gene decided that he could assume greater career risks on behalf of his company. He resolved to

- Propose an HRD program that would respond directly to a *strategic business need*, not just to a *management want*
- Include a *forecast of the financial benefit* of this HRD program in his proposal to management and agree to *evaluate the actual benefit* of the program at its conclusion

Both of these actions took some courage. Both were clearly outside Gene's generally recognized professional strengths, and both were departures from current HRD practice. To be honest, though, any real risk to Gene's career was mitigated somewhat by his private resolve to seek employment elsewhere unless some expansion of his role in his company was forthcoming.

Gene's company had lost a significant percentage of its market share to a new competitor. After the board of directors had studied the company's annual business plans and reported its observations of various operations throughout the company, it concluded that improved customer service could significantly improve sales volume. The directors agreed with Gene that a major HRD effort to alter the present corporate approach to customer service was required. Gene's investigation yielded the following forecast figures for the proposed customer-service program:

Performance value	$200,000
– Cost	50,000
Benefit	$150,000

The forecast benefit was significant. A 4-to-1 return on investment for the HRD program could be realized in twelve months. With such figures in hand, Gene easily gained support for the proposed customer-service HRD program. Because Gene used extremely conservative estimates for his calculations, it was no surprise to him that the actual return on investment at the conclusion of the program was 8 to 1, or a $400,000 performance value for a $50,000 investment. Almost overnight, Gene moved into the inner circle of decision makers in his firm.

Gene has become convinced that two different views of the expected results of HRD can be blended into one powerful HRD package. He has not lost his traditional "people-skills" of HRD. In fact, his ideas about human development are more widely shared among the people in his firm than ever before as a result of their being exposed to the content of the customer-service program. Although his new economic perspective on the "human capital" of the firm might have been less than characteristic of his thinking a short time ago, he now talks about human resources as worthy of investment. He believes that the smart business invests in and takes care of its people. Gene talks with ease to management about these things in their own language—the language of dollars and cents— every time he proposes an HRD program.

Opportunity

The opportunity to talk about the financial costs and benefits of HRD is available to every HRD professional. In Gene Williams's case, the pressure to change came from within himself. In other instances, the pressure to change may come from management or from peers. In our experience, the pressure for financial results comes from the top as executives begin to ask their HRD staff what real value their department is contributing to the organization. Interestingly, and fortunately for HRD, these same executives hold relatively modest expectations for HRD's adding value to the company. Working in such circumstances of high pressure and low expectations leads the HRD staff to ask, "We know what HRD can do for our company, but will management believe any forecast benefit greater than a 2-to-1 return on investment?" To deal with this practical concern, we must move on to discuss the benefit computation and then consider how to present proposals to management.

Benefit Computation

The benefit computation is a simple subtraction activity recorded on the Benefit Analysis Worksheet (Exhibit 20).

Positive Benefits. Benefit figures can be examined from several perspectives. The first is to note if the calculated benefit is a positive one. Does the performance value of the proposed HRD program exceed the total costs of the program? Breaking even is acceptable; anything more is gravy. A forecast benefit of a 1-to-1 measurable return on an HRD investment can represent value to the organization. If the forecast for performance value and cost is made conservatively, there is always the potential for a return greater than 1 to 1. Furthermore, many HRD programs also can be expected to yield such nonfinancial benefits to the organization as strengthening the culture and encouraging a better understanding of its traditions.

Relative Benefits. When two or more HRD options are available to address a performance problem, the forecast financial benefit model offers an easy method for deciding between them. The following figures will illustrate this point:

Exhibit 20. Benefit Analysis Worksheet.

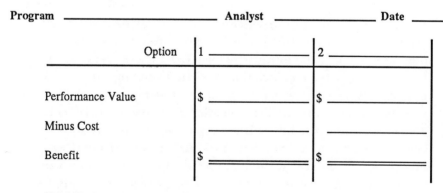

Program _____ Analyst _____ Date _____

	Option	1 _____	2 _____
Performance Value		$ _____	$ _____
Minus Cost		_____	_____
Benefit		$ _____	$ _____

Note: Circle your choice of option.

	Unstructured Option 1	*Structured Option 2*	*Structured Option 3*
Performance Value	$90,000	$288,000	$225,000
– Costs	0	100,000	150,000
Benefit	$90,000	$188,000	$ 75,000

If we were to look only at the proposed financial benefits, option 2 would clearly be the best investment choice. The forecast benefit of $188,000 can be compared directly with the forecast benefit of $90,000 for option 1 and $75,000 for option 3. In a cash-short organization, however, the relatively small advantage of option 1, the unstructured HRD program, over option 3, a structured program, will appear quite attractive. Because unstructured HRD incurs no direct costs, it will not cut into already limited cash resources. Furthermore, unstructured HRD requires little or no change in organizational operations.

Return on Investment. The third perspective is to review the return on investment, which is simply a ratio that expresses the relationship of every dollar of performance value to every dollar expended to achieve that value. The return on investment for each option is obtained by dividing the forecast performance value by the forecast cost. If not otherwise stated, we assume that return on investment is based on a one-year period. For example, a 2-to-1 ratio means that $2 are returned for every $1 invested in a program in a one-year period. Most forecasts will be based on the longest HRD option under scrutiny. The returns on investment for our three options are:

- Option 1, none ($0 invested)
- Option 2, 2.88 to 1
- Option 3, 1.5 to 1

By calculating returns on investment, we can compare the return from a $1 investment in each alternative action to achieve performance goals. In this way, investments in human resources can be compared with each other and with investments in new machinery, new work methods, or other performance improvement efforts.

Decisions Based on Finances

With your numbers in hand, decision makers can choose among all options under consideration. This is a fairly straightforward task. They simply choose the option that has the greatest financial benefit. But wait just a minute! We are compelled to offer the following advice to help you and the decision makers in your company maintain perspective.

Wild Figures. Many HRD managers are afraid that they will come up with a crazy, inaccurate forecast. We urge you to note that it is the correctness of the decision, not the accuracy of the figures themselves, that counts. Granted, the accuracy of the figures and the correctness of the decision are related, but there remains some leeway for the forecaster. If all your forecast figures could be accurate to the penny, choosing among options would be easy. While this ideal state is not to be found in the real world, our research has demonstrated that inaccurate figures are less of a threat to making correct decisions than you might think.

How can this be? The reason is simple. Again and again through many studies, we have found it reasonable to rely on the internal consistency of individual forecasters. Conservative forecasters, on the one hand, consistently forecast low benefits for the options they are considering. Liberal forecasters, on the other hand, consistently forecast high benefits for the options they are considering. The relative consistency, not the precision, of each forecaster's figures is the key. For the same proposed HRD program, three forecasters may find different benefits figures and still arrive at the same program decision. The following example will demonstrate what we mean by internal consistency and how the decision maker might have a high level of confidence in making the correct decision even when given a variety of financial benefit forecasts. The following benefits for three HRD options were prepared by two forecasters:

	Option 1	Option 2	Option 3
Forecaster A	$70,000	$150,000	$170,000
Forecaster B	$50,000	$100,000	$125,000

The benefit figures from either forecaster will lead decision makers to choose option 3.

Along with our confidence in the essential rightness of such decisions, we offer an important caution: The acceptance of some variability in benefit figures should not lead you to think that we condone casual inventions of costs and performance value figures. It was clear that the forecasters in our research studies had gathered their figures with serious intent and had made their forecasts with care. It is this serious approach to the task that ensures the internal consistency of the figures developed by each forecaster.

Unstructured HRD. The issue of the relative accuracy of forecast figures is very important to organizational strategists and planners who want answers to the following questions:

- How can we assure the greatest return on our available capital?
- Given various options, which one will we choose?

In Chapters Two and Three we noted that there is no such thing as no HRD. We defined HRD as consisting of programs meant to enhance the organization's capabilities for reaching planned goals. We included in our definition the possibility of affecting changes in expertise, aptitude, motivation, and work design through HRD. Most managers believe that they are already effectively enhancing the capabilities of people in their firms. But in our experience, the most inept managers have zero-cost programs, which they justify by telling themselves, "Our people develop on the job." These managers little realize the effects of their HRD programs, or the lack of them, on their workers and on their company's ability to compete in the marketplace. We call this approach to the problem of development *unstructured HRD*, or the unplanned process for obtaining expertise, aptitude, motivation, and work design through accident, acts of God, and the goodwill of employees. Whenever and wherever unstructured HRD exists in an organization, it is *essential* that you gather base-line figures so that unstructured HRD can be compared with the forecast results of structured programs. Revealing the financial benefits figures of existing unstructured HRD will help in answering the question, Which is the best HRD option? (By convention, we generally place the ongoing unstructured option in column 1 of each worksheet.)

Nonfinancial Criteria

So far, we have focused on the financial benefits of investing in HRD because we believe that a general lack of expertise in forecasting and evaluating the financial benefits of programs is a major block to making good organizational investments in HRD. Still, we realize that even without this forecasting expertise, HRD professionals have been doing quite well. Obviously, criteria other than financial ones are being used for choosing HRD programs from among the available options.

We have identified six criteria to use when comparing and choosing among HRD options:

- *Appropriateness* to the organizational culture and tradition
- *Availability* of the program
- Perceived *quality* of the program design
- *Prior effectiveness* of the same or a similar program
- *Cost* of the program
- Expected *financial benefit* to the organization

Financial benefit is only one of the criteria for choosing a particular option. Then, too, decision makers may not use all six criteria for making every HRD program decision. Nor will they always weight each criterion equally.

We have talked about forecasting costs primarily as a means to calculating the benefits of HRD programs. We realize, however, that many organizations have a limited amount of available working capital and that staying within a limited budget may be mandatory, no matter what the expected benefit of a structured HRD program is. To propose that decision makers invest in HRD programs that are beyond current organizational resources is a lot like asking a poor man with $10 to his name to invest $10,000 on the promise of becoming a millionaire. His reach toward his fortune must begin with a $10 investment—and no more.

The first two criteria listed above—appropriateness and availability—depend on the context in which they are applied. Applying a criterion of appropriateness to the organizational culture and tradition helps the HRD professional think about alternative HRD programs in terms of their goodness of fit. Clearly, some programs that would fail in one organization might succeed in another. Such variables as appropriateness of content, method, presenter, and location must be taken into consideration.

The second criterion, availability, is primarily a question of logistics. Dates, time of day, and locations for program delivery are often either critical or mandated. If a program option is not available when needed, clearly it must be dropped from consideration.

The two quality criteria of program design and prior effectiveness of the program also aid in valuing the options being considered. The program design criterion is used to evaluate the general strategy and the major elements of the program, as well as its potential for meeting the original, carefully defined organizational need. Unfortunately, it is too often simply assumed that this criterion has been met. Among an array of programs, some designs are more likely to meet the performance need than are others.

To satisfy the second quality criterion, effectiveness, the HRD professional must deliberately seek evidence of the prior effectiveness of the same or similar programs delivered by the providers of the programs under consideration.

Table 1 demonstrates the usefulness of a two-axis matrix as a decision aid. The selection criteria are placed on one axis and the HRD options under consideration on the other. In our sample decision matrix the six criteria are equally weighted for options A through D. Each option is ranked from 1 (best) to 4 (worst) on each of the selection criteria. The *lowest* score indicates best choice. According to our example, option B is the one to choose. Taking the same situation and increasing the importance of some of the criteria by weighting them would result in other preferred options.

Table 1. HRD Selection Decision Matrix.

Decision Criteria	HRD Program Options			
	A	*B*	*C*	*D*
1. Appropriateness to culture and tradition	3	2	4	1
2. Availability (date/time/place)	1	2	4	3
3. Quality: Program design	1	2	3	4
4. Quality: Prior effectiveness	2	1	3	4
5. Financial: Benefit	4	1	2	3
6. Financial: Cost	4	3	1	2
Totals	15	11	17	17

Note: Rank each option on each criteria: 1 = highest, 4 = lowest.

The ultimate choice will come from a combination of the facts, the intuition of decision makers, and their willingness to take risks. Making your own choice among the available options is one thing. Management's choosing among the available options is another. In the remainder of this chapter we discuss the problem of presenting your proposal to management.

Presenting Your Proposal to Management

The purpose of this section is to help you gain management's approval for your HRD program proposal. We assume that your proposed program is meant to respond to a carefully determined performance need and that it is appropriate to your organization's culture. Unless it is designed to meet these two criteria, you will have little, if any, ammunition with which to defend it against its critics or against other, non-HRD options. In addition, you must skillfully present your program proposal to management.

At a minimum, most HRD proposals must contain four major elements:

- Performance need
- Program goal

- Program options
- Program recommendation

Performance Need. The performance need is a carefully determined and desired change in worker, work-group, or organizational performance. The need can be expressed in the form of a performance goal or a performance deficiency, either of which should be central to the mission of the organization.

Program Goal. Progress toward the work performance goal in question will probably be influenced by both HRD and non-HRD factors. Changing the reward system is an example of a non-HRD program that could be instituted along with an HRD program. Whenever a parallel non-HRD program will be instituted to cope with the same performance goal, the HRD program goal will typically be smaller in scope than the identified organizational goal or the total performance deficiency. Adjusting HRD program goals to the realities of the situation is critical to establishing long-term credibility for HRD. Promising outcomes that cannot be delivered will only cause problems for the HRD department down the road. So promise what you know you can deliver and on occasion, surprise yourself and management with more than you promised.

Program Options. The third element of a proposal involves presentation of reasonable HRD program options. The purpose of this element is to allow decision makers a choice or to make your case for the single best HRD program.

Program Recommendation. The fourth element is your recommendation to management to approve what is in your opinion the best HRD program option. Here is where you must stand on your own two feet. You are prepared to make a persuasive argument; you are also prepared to risk rejection.

We cannot overemphasize the idea that good performance needs assessments are essential if genuine performance needs and the strategic performance goals of your company are to be identified. Important performance needs and goals are the basis for responsible HRD programs and for sound financial forecasting of program benefits. You might want to consult Kaufman (1986) and Mager (1970), who provide advice on conducting needs assessments. You should also understand that there are both good and bad needs assessments and that good ones are not necessarily lengthy or complicated. Unfortunately, too many HRD experts would lead you to believe that this is the case.

Rules for Presenting Your Proposal

Our advice for preparing HRD proposals for presentation has been kept to a minimum. We advocate four short rules for the presentation itself:

- Keep it simple.
- Present visual and verbal information in your proposal.
- Talk to the person(s) with authority.
- Strive for believability.

Because presentation situations vary, the above rules are not listed in the order of their importance. You should consider the circumstances of your presentations and order these rules accordingly.

Keep It Simple. Simplicity is both beautiful and illusive. Most of us take pleasure in hearing important thoughts presented concisely, clearly, and with their fullness intact. Most of us know when we see or hear elegant simplicity. And yet, we have to struggle to achieve elegant simplicity in our own efforts. Simple ideas—right or wrong—are generally more acceptable to people than complex ideas. But keeping your presentation simple without losing the integrity of the idea is the hard part. In the short run, complexity will be the easier path to take. In the long run, making the extra effort to achieve simplicity will provide a larger payoff.

Because simplicity is one of the strengths of the HRD benefit-forecasting method, be careful not to lose this simplicity at the proposal stage. We know some HRD managers who cannot resist telling everything they know when they present their proposals to management. They seem to think that reporting all their hard work will gain them the approval they seek. What it will gain them is a sympathy vote. People in the fund-raising business talk about getting "go-away money." You want more than that. We have provided you with a simple model and a simple framework for your proposal. Do not abandon this elegant simplicity for confusing complexity when you make your presentation to management.

The twin aspects of your presentation are the HRD benefit-forecasting model (performance value minus cost equals benefit) and the HRD program proposal (performance need, performance goal, program options, and program recommendation). Both of these aspects of your presentation should be anchored in the performance issue you have chosen to address, since performance is essential to achieving the fundamental business goals of your company. This kind of approach will lead to your receiving approval for your HRD proposal.

Visual and Verbal. The saying that "a picture is worth a thousand words" certainly holds true for visually oriented people. For the nonvisual, a picture may be worth less than this, but it will always be worth something. In any organization, some management people will be verbal, some visual, and some both. The point is that you seek approval from a variety of types of people. Why gamble? We advise you to use both verbal and visual symbols when you present your proposal. And, yes, keep them simple.

To the visual and verbal aspects specified above, we add the following two considerations: First, should you present your proposal in person or in the form of a written proposal, or should you use both methods? Second, should you present the majority of your ideas through the written word, through graphic illustrations, or both?

As a seeker of management approval, you have everything to gain by helping decision makers understand what it is that you are proposing. What good does it do to explain at some later time, "I put all that information in the report—if only they had read it"? This necessity for communicating proposals in so many dimensions causes outsiders to shudder at the difficulties of business communication. But such is your task. Your HRD proposal should elicit from management a common vision of the HRD program, in spite of the fact that achieving this goal can make creative writing and film making seem easy. The presentation strategies are as follows:

1. Address each of the four simple proposal elements.
2. Use the benefit-forecasting method.
3. In making a written proposal, use concise sentences and paragraphs.
4. When appearing in person: present your information in the same order as your on-paper proposal and at a pace preferred by your audience.
5. Use one or two visuals, such as the performance-time graph or the forecasting figures, to illustrate the benefit expected to result from the program. These visuals can be sketched on napkins if you present your proposal over a cup of coffee in the cafeteria or on transparencies if you present it in the boardroom.
6. In your written proposal include the visuals cited above and consider adding other easily understood graphic information, such as performance charts showing sales production, turn-over, absenteeism, scrap, and rework.

Authority. If necessary, first take a deep breath and then approach the appropriate decision maker with your proposal. Of course, we assume that you will respect the need to go through channels and to attend to corporate etiquette. Who has the authority to make the decision that you seek and who cares about the strategic business need that you propose to address with an HRD program? It is important to build business alliances with all the people you contact on the way to reaching the decision maker from whom you need approval. Of course, by giving such advice, we are really asking you to take even more risks.

Nonrisk takers are easy to spot. Everywhere we go in most organizations, we hear bitter stories about their having had the same idea for which someone else is getting credit. An unpresented proposal is a nonproposal. The proposal that is presented by someone who is not familiar with it or committed to it will surely be watered down or relegated to the nearest pile of documents "on hold." Our advice to you is to make the presentation yourself and to the right people.

Believability. Our most important piece of advice concerns the relative believability of your proposal. We have already discussed top management's inclination to pressure HRD to contribute more to the organization while it simultaneously has little confidence in HRD's capacity to do so. Your estimate of the true benefits to be obtained from a proposed program may exceed top management's willingness to believe that estimate for any number of reasons. Top managers want to work in partnership with HRD, just as they do with other organizational functions. But when managers have more alternatives before them than they can approve, believability becomes an issue. Thus, any facts in your presentation that clearly fall outside the realm of reason or the experience of the decision makers will be ignored or discounted. Decision makers will tend to assume that you are lying to them or trying to trick them. Our advice is to consider working within a "window of believability." What do you suppose will happen if you come along and say, "We can net an 800 percent return on investment in six months." Will the decision makers believe your proposal? What is the minimum return on investment that will gain their support? What is the maximum return on investment they will consider feasible? Let's say your group of decision makers believes that their investing in HRD could be a break-even proposition and that the maximum potential yield is $2.50 for every $1 invested. What will you do if your most conservative financial benefit forecast is in the neighborhood of $8 for every $1 invested? The HRD consultants who use the benefit-forecasting method tell us that when a proposed return on investment falls outside management's window of believability, it will be swiftly rejected. In such a case a forecast return on investment of "at least 2 to 1" will probably be quite attractive and far more acceptable. On occasion we have recommended to one large HRD department that it establish a practice of promising at least a 2-to-1 return on investment regardless of the fact that the calculated benefits actually exceed this goal. Because the department's actual return-on-investment record has been much better than $2 for every $1 invested in HRD, it feels quite safe in presenting its proposals to management. Believability is an important consideration in gaining approval.

Summary

The purpose of this chapter was to develop an understanding of benefit analysis and skill in presenting HRD proposals to management. Beyond the basic financial forecasting model, which yields the dollar benefit, we offered alternative ways of expressing the benefit:

- Positive benefit for each option under consideration
- Relative benefit among options
- Return on investment projected for each option

We discussed two bases for choosing the best HRD program option:

- Financial
- Nonfinancial

We also emphasized that the purpose of presenting proposals to management is to gain approval for them, and we discussed the four elements of a proposal:

- Performance need
- Performance goal
- Program options
- Program recommendation

Finally, we noted that, in presenting your proposal, you should keep it simple, use both visual and verbal methods, seek out those in your organization who have real authority, and make sure that your figures are believable.

We have seen HRD managers who at this point run away from the opportunity to make greater contributions to their organizations. We have also seen those who jump headfirst into the deepest part of the pool. Both responses represent amateurish overreactions to new information. Practice must come before confidence. If you are considering the "run-away" response, we offer the following observation: *Do not underestimate the power of this simple forecasting tool for communicating with management and thus gaining their approval for responsible HRD programs.*

It is important to understand the relationship between what you do and the benefits you produce. Do not underestimate the importance of knowing your value to your company. The financial forecasting model can help you identify worthy activities and select the option having the greatest benefit, and you can then go on to develop programs with confidence in their worth to your company.

8

++

Case Examples
of Benefit Analysis
and Presentation

This chapter of cases provides illustrations of benefit analysis and of the presentation of the forecast information to decision makers in an organization. Again, we review the same five cases that were presented in Chapters Four and Six—manufacturing, service industry, organization development, management, and public sector.

Manufacturing

The manufacturing case focused on the problem of an unacceptably high rejection rate of expensive electronic circuit boards during their production. Structured technical training for production workers was determined to be an appropriate HRD response to this problem. Three HRD options were entertained in the forecast. They include keeping the existing unstructured on-the-job training, using an HRD consultant who specializes in electronics technical training, and developing a training program using in-house personnel.

From a strictly financial perspective, it is clear that the forecast benefit of $180,000 for the existing unstructured training option is unacceptable when compared to the forecast benefit of $265,800 for the consultant option and of $252,144 for the in-house development option (Exhibit 21).

From a benefits-only perspective, the in-house option offers only $13,656 less in benefit to the organization than does the consultant option. This relatively insignificant difference leaves room

Exhibit 21. Benefit Analysis Worksheet.

Program	Circuit Boards		Analyst	B. Lawther		Date	5/8/88

Option	1	Unstructured	2	In-House	3	Consultant
Performance Value	$	180,000	$	270,000	$	288,000
Minus Cost		0		17,856		22,200
Benefit	$	180,000	$	252,144	$	265,800

Note: Circle your choice of option.

to consider the other five HRD decision criteria—appropriateness, availability, quality, prior effectiveness, and cost—for choosing the best option. In this case, the prior effectiveness and availability decision criteria emerged as issues. The managers were generally unimpressed with the consultant because he could provide little evidence of the prior effectiveness of his program. They were also concerned about his ability to deliver high-quality training in the midst of an already heavy client load. Given these concerns, the decision makers chose the in-house option.

Service Industry

The service industry case demonstrates what happens in an organization that has let its HRD efforts slip over the years. Now the service company will have to hire twenty-five new employees to execute badly needed market analyses. Three options—unstructured, vendor-delivered, and in-house HRD—were considered in response to the immediate performance need of this organization.

The benefit forecast definitely seemed to favor the vendor option. The forecast clearly eliminated the low-cost, low-benefit unstructured option from consideration (Exhibit 22). The forecast $45,411 difference in benefits between the vendor option and the in-house option is significant. Decision makers would have to see some

Exhibit 22. Benefit Analysis Worksheet.

| Program | _Market Analysis_ | | Analyst | _L. Swenson_ | Date | _4/30/88_ |

Option	1	_Unstructured_	2	_Vendor_	3	_In-House_
Performance Value	$	_210,000_	$	_378,000_	$	_322,000_
Minus Cost		_5,000_		_25,290_		_14,701_
Benefit	$	_205,000_	$	_352,710_	$	_307,299_

Note: Circle your choice of option.

impressive gain from the five other decision criteria in order to reject this benefit. If there had been a critical problem of vendor availability, for example, the in-house option would have been the better option. Delaying the development of twenty-five new hires is nearly unthinkable in a profit-making organization.

Organization Development

The forecast benefits in the organization development case offer quite a contrast. The costs are within $9,000 of each other, but the benefits differ by $87,000 (Exhibit 23). This is, however, not just an issue of economic benefit. The consultant promises to deliver a fairly standard HRD customer service program. Likewise, the consultant's program promises to have a relatively low impact on organizational performance. In contrast, the in-house version promises to significantly alter corporate values as they relate to the importance of customers. The program is intended to challenge every employee to develop a "sense of the customer" that has been lacking in the organization. It offers much greater risk and rewards than the consultant's program. Decision makers must choose be-tween two very different strategies. Which is more appropriate to

Exhibit 23. Benefit Analysis Worksheet.

Program _____Customer Service_____   Analyst _____B. Webb_____   Date _3/15/88_

	Option	1 In-House	2 Consultant
Performance Value		$ 280,000	$ 50,000
Minus Cost		24,000	15,000
Benefit		$ 256,000	$ 35,000

Note: Circle your choice of option.

the performance need? Given their competitive situation, the decision makers took the riskier option to change the organization's culture.

Management Development

The management case is a classic "go/no-go" situation. The organization's project management problems give the appearance of continuing for some time. Staying with the current situation will bring no added performance value, no cost, and no gain—in contrast to a proposed redesigned work system that costs $21,000 but will bring $150,000 in performance value gain and thus a benefit of $129,000 (Exhibit 24).

The company is not in financial crisis, even though aspects of the current situation are chaotic. For this reason, the decision criteria of appropriateness, quality, and prior effectiveness will dominate the decision process. New work systems have in the past backfired in this organization, so the decision makers want assurances that the new work system will, in fact, work better.

Public Sector

The public sector case described an auditing and collection agency whose new staff had previously required fifteen months of

Exhibit 24. Benefit Analysis Worksheet.

Program ___*Project Management*___   Analyst ___*C.A.S.*___   Date ___*7/1/88*___

	Option	1 *Unstructured*	2 *Project Mgt.*
Performance Value		$ 0	$ 150,000
Minus Cost		0	21,000
Benefit		$ 0	$ 129,000

Note: Circle your choice of option.

field experience to reach competency. A program to teach coaching skills to experienced staff to use when working with the new staff was determined to be an appropriate method for shortening the process of developing new staff. The forecaster looked at two options—the existing fifteen-month development program and a new thirteen-month structured option. Exhibit 25 presents the benefit analysis for both programs. From a strictly financial perspective, the structured program would appear to be by far the most desirable—$2,566,335 in benefit versus only $2,283,750 for the existing program. The other five decision criteria of appropriateness, availability, quality, prior effectiveness, and cost would also need to be applied before recommending a program choice to decision makers. In this instance, the up-front cost of the program with the highest benefit was the only serious consideration. The agency was on a fixed budget and would have to make an appeal to a special government agency to fund this effort. Nevertheless, the structured program was supported by the decision makers because of its forecast benefit.

Summary

If you are ready to dive into the pool, we advise you to back off for a while. We suggest that you *start with a noncontroversial*

Exhibit 25. Benefit Analysis Worksheet.

Program _____Coaching Skills_____ Analyst ___C. Sleezer___ Date ___3/1/88___

		Option	1	Unstructured	2	NAA Course
Performance Value			$	2,283,750	$	2,613,750
Minus Cost				0		47,415
Benefit			$	2,283,750	$	2,566,335

Note: Circle your choice of option.

project or consider keeping your first-time-ever forecast to yourself. Professionals learning any new skill have enough challenge without choosing a difficult project. Later, when you have practiced and gained expertise, you can apply the HRD financial forecasting method to a controversial or highly visible project in your company. But first try the method out on small, low-risk HRD programs. Develop a "feel" for the process and learn the analytical thinking skills that are essential to using the financial forecasting model. Don't forget that you are likely to encounter politics related to company financial matters with which you need to become familiar. Becoming an expert takes time.

The rest is up to you. Run away? We hope not. Dive into the deep end first? We hope not. We suggest that you practice, practice, and then practice some more. In Chapter Nine you will find several cases on which to practice using the Performance Value and Cost Analysis worksheets and presenting HRD facts by way of the financial forecasting method.

9

✛✛✛✛✛✛✛✛✛✛✛✛✛✛✛✛✛✛✛✛✛✛✛✛✛✛✛✛✛✛✛✛✛✛✛✛

Using Financial
Forecasting Tools

A secret to understanding is doing. The following pages contain two fairly simple exercises, along with a more complicated one. They will give you the opportunity to practice using the financial benefit forecasting method. This is your chance to feel the sense of power that can result from forecasting the benefits of HRD programs.

Unlike the situations you will find in the real world, we have conveniently supplied in each case all the information you need to use the forecasting method. On the job, you would have had to do a lot of digging to get the same kind of information. In each case, we have left out any extraneous or false information or indications of company politics, all of which could be present and important when you are gathering information for making HRD decisions in your company. We have aggregated many of the costs of HRD programs and thus have lost some of the details of costing. This simplifies the forecasting task, but it will not change any of your conclusions. Your job is to accept the facts as they are given in each case. Assume that the options provided are the only viable ones and that each option will deliver the promised performance.

Before you begin, we offer the following tested rules for completing the exercises:

1. As you read each exercise, underline or highlight important information.

Note: You do not need permission from the publisher to copy blank forms following p. 152. In fact, we have included them precisely so that you can easily reproduce and use them yourself.

2. Make several copies of the Performance-Time Graph, as well as the Performance Value, Cost Analysis, and Benefit Analysis worksheets. (You will find blank forms later in this chapter.)
3. Use a sharp pencil with a good eraser. Even with extra forms, you will need to erase. Trust us.
4. Use a calculator for the arithmetic. Save your effort for analyzing options and applying the facts of the case to the logic of the forms.
5. Do the first two exercises before beginning the third one. You will need to rely on some of the techniques you practiced on the first two to complete the third.
6. Fill in the Performance-Time Graph and the Performance Value Worksheet before completing the Cost Analysis Worksheet and Benefit Analysis worksheet.
7. For each exercise, work through one option at a time. This will help prevent mix-ups.
8. Turn negative numbers into positive numbers, which are much easier to work with.
9. Be persistent. Don't look at the answers before you have completed each exercise. The answers can be found at the end of the chapter.
10. Finally, review the answers for each exercise. Make sure you understand where all of the data came from and how each calculation was made.

Exercise 1: Delivery Service

Situation. You are the HRD manager for Metro Tribune, Inc., the publisher of a daily newspaper. The paper is delivered seven days a week, mostly by school-age carriers. Their adult supervisors have lately been fielding many complaints from readers about missing papers. Upon reviewing company records for the past year, you find that in the first month on the job new carriers deliver an average of only six papers per week to each of their one hundred customers. Most new carriers need about four weeks of experience to reach the full performance rate of seven delivered papers per customer per week. Meanwhile, Metro's customers are permitted to delete 50 cents per undelivered paper from their payments each week. A quick needs assessment shows that new carriers lack the expertise to perform their work to the expected standard. Next week you anticipate that a batch of 100 newly hired carriers will start their routes. You estimate that a very simple training session and a job aid for carriers to use during their first week on the job will result in no missed deliveries as of one week after their training. The costs for the proposed training program include: $80 for job analysis, $120 for the trainer's salary while developing the training session and job aid, $20 to photocopy the job aid, $40 for evaluating the program, and $100 for prizes to be given as incentives to come to the training session. Parents will transport their children to the session. You can rent the local school auditorium for $200 for the day, and you plan no refreshments because the school principal explicitly asked you not to bring food or beverages into the building.

Directions. Your job as a forecaster is to use the Performance-Time Graph to sketch a picture of the situation or to go right to the Performance Value Worksheet. First figure the performance value and the cost of the existing unstructured training situation (option 1). Then figure the performance value and the cost of the structured training program (option 2). Compare the two options by finding the benefit for each and, finally, circle the option that yields the most benefit for the organization.

Exercise 2: Skill Training

Situation. You are the plant manager of a manufacturing company where workers will install three new fabricating machines next month. Each machine is capable of producing sixty parts per day, provided the operator knows how to run the machine. Each completed part made to specifications is worth $10.

You want to know if you will achieve a financial benefit for your company in thirty working days if you send three operators who have had no previous experience with the new machines to the factory school for training. Another option would be to ask the operators to review the printed training materials that come with the machines and learn to operate the new machines on the job. You expect the operators to be fully competent at the conclusion of either program.

The cost of sending the operators to the factory school for four days is $2,000 per operator, including travel and lodging. However, your company does not regularly assign any costs to on-the-job training. The operators have scanned the manual for the new machines and believe that with some practice, they can be fully operational in thirty working days.

Directions. Your job as forecaster is to complete the Performance-Time Graph and the worksheets and then decide whether or not to send the three operators to the factory training school. In the past, you have not viewed such expenditures for training with enthusiasm.

Exercise 3: Management Development

Situation. You are part of an organization that does engineering systems design. The company is a leader in its field. About a year ago, it created a project engineering department so that all ten project engineers could be brought together in one location rather than work out of several divisions. The purpose of the change was to allow the project engineers to focus on concept development for projects. The project engineers were expected to spend more time managing the design engineers and less time pursuing those technical activities that could easily be handled by the design engineers. The project engineering department is headed by an executive with an outstanding record in project management.

Unfortunately, since the project engineering department was established, the company has experienced an alarming turnover of design engineers. A performance needs assessment revealed that the project engineers were experiencing certain difficulties in managing the design engineers who report to them. The project engineers lack expertise in communicating direction, delegating responsibilities, and handling crises. Data from exit interviews revealed that the inability of project engineers to manage crises and to establish clear guidelines and directions was the primary cause of the frustration felt by the design engineers who quit. The performance needs assessment also confirmed that creating the project engineering department had been a reasonably good decision because communication about new design concepts among the project engineers has been greatly enhanced.

The turnover problem has had a large financial impact on the company. It costs approximately $75,000 to find, hire, and relocate a design engineer with the appropriate credentials and experience. In the last nine months, the company has had to replace five design engineers. At this rate you are justified in anticipating that the company will replace a total of six design engineers before the end of another year. You have been asked to recommend an HRD program to address the managerial deficiencies of the project engineers. The goal is to reduce the turnover among the design engineers from six to two per year.

Your HRD options are to send each of the project engineers to a management development institute that was recommended by a senior executive, arrange for a vendor-delivered management program, or begin a coaching program to help the project engineers develop the management expertise they need. Your director has suggested that the last option could take as long as ten months to achieve the desired results. The probability is extremely low that the project engineers will develop the expertise they need informally, on the job. Your company does not consider salaries or other normal daily employee costs to be part of HRD costs. It will provide a budget of $7,000 for materials and $20,000 for a consultant to support the coaching approach to the problem.

The vendor-supplied management development program would involve fifteen four-hour sessions to be delivered on site over a six-month period. It would cost $15,000 per participant and could start immediately. Next, the management development institute would deliver an eighty-hour program off site over a two-week period. This program would cost $10,000 per participant, including airfare, lodging, food, and materials. The next program at the institute begins in two weeks.

The last option is the coaching program. Here, the consultant's fee would be $20,000, to be split as follows:

- Needs assessment (50 percent)
- Work analysis (25 percent)
- Program evaluation and report (25 percent)

The total budget for materials for the coaching option would be $7,000, to be split as follows:

- Needs analysis (10 percent)
- Work analysis (5 percent)
- Design (5 percent)
- Development (15 percent)
- Implementation (50 percent)
- Evaluation (15 percent)

The coaching program could begin immediately.

Follow the same method in completing this program as you did in using the method to forecast the benefit in exercises 1 and 2. Remember, your units of work should be stated in positive numbers. When you figure the development time, make sure you figure it from the actual start of the program. Make sure all time units are the same for all options. Finally, it is permitted to talk about partial engineers because you are dealing with the value of the engineer, not his or her person.

Summary

Applying economic tools to everyday business decisions sometimes leads to unexpected results. The same is true for HRD. The honest HRD practitioner may have to admit that some favorite, well-attended, or faddish programs will contribute few financial benefits to the organization and that some practical, pedestrian, difficult, or innovative programs will contribute enormous benefits to the profits or the future viability of the organization.

If you have not talked in economic terms about the benefits of HRD, we will wager that management in your organization does not know the true value of its HRD activities. When you share your knowledge of forecasting financial benefits and when decision makers fully understand the real and potential value of HRD programs and activities, they are likely to turn into believers and supporters of the department. Further, they will begin to realize the full potential of HRD as a competitive tool. Be forewarned that decision makers could also begin to watch the activities of your department more closely. If this possibility causes you some concern, remember that you can use the financial forecasting method to help you manage your department better. You can discover the power to evaluate HRD solutions and alternatives that you had previously only assumed would be economically beneficial. You can decide or help decide where to cut back on HRD in lean times. You can request a larger, more realistic budget when circumstances call for greater use of HRD. You can rest assured that your contributions to the well-being of your organization will be recognized.

When you are able to forecast and present the benefits of HRD programs with assurance, you need not fear the prospect of assuming greater accountability for your department and your work.

Figure 5. Performance-Time Graph.

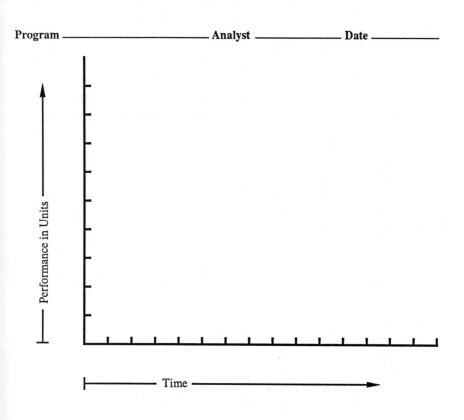

Exhibit 26. Performance Value Worksheet.

Note that performance units and time units for all options must remain consistent throughout the forecast.

Program _____ Analyst _____ Date _____

	Option name	1	2
Data required for calculations:			
(a) What **unit** of work performance are you measuring?		_____ unit name	_____ unit name
(b) What is the performance goal per worker/work group at the **end** of the HRD program?		_____ / _____ no. units / time	_____ / _____ no. units / time
(c) What is the performance per worker/work group at the **beginning** of the HRD program?		_____ / _____ no. units / time	_____ / _____ no. units / time
(d) What **dollar value** is assigned to each performance unit?		$ _____ / unit	$ _____ / unit
(e) What is the **development time** required to reach the expected performance level?		_____ _____ no. time	_____ _____ no. time
(f) What is the **evaluation period**? (Enter the longest time (e) of all options being considered.)		_____ _____ no. time	_____ _____ no. time
(g) How many workers/work groups will **participate** in the HRD program?		_____ no. workers/groups	_____ no. workers/groups

Calculations to determine net performance value:

	(Option 1)	(Option 2)
(h) Will worker/work group produce **usable units** during the HRD program? If no, enter -0-. If yes, enter known performance rate or calculate average performance rate. $[(b + c)/2]$	no. _____ units	no. _____ units
(i) What total units per worker/work group will be produced during the **development time**? $(h \times e)$	_____ no. of units	_____ no. of units
(j) How many units will be produced per worker/work group during the **evaluation period**? $\{[(f - e) \times b] + i\}$	_____ no. of units	_____ no. of units
(k) What will be the value of the worker's/work group's performance during the **evaluation period**? $(j \times d)$	$ _____	$ _____
(l) What is the performance value gain per worker/work group? $[k - (c \times d \times f)]$	$ _____	$ _____
(m) What is the total performance value gain for all workers/work groups? $(l \times g)$	$ _____	$ _____

Exhibit 27. Cost Analysis Worksheet.

Program _____ Analyst _____ Date _____

Option name	1 _____	2 _____
Analysis:		
Needs assessment	_____	_____
Work analysis	_____	_____
Proposal to management	_____	_____
Other _____	_____	_____
Other _____	_____	_____
Design:		
General HRD program design	_____	_____
Specific HRD program design	_____	_____
Other _____	_____	_____
Other _____	_____	_____
Development:		
Draft and prototype	_____	_____
Pilot test and revise	_____	_____
Production and duplication	_____	_____
Other _____	_____	_____
Other _____	_____	_____
Implement:		
Program management	_____	_____
Program delivery	_____	_____
Participant costs	_____	_____
Other _____	_____	_____
Other _____	_____	_____
Evaluation:		
Program evaluation and report	_____	_____
Performance follow-up	_____	_____
Other _____	_____	_____
Other _____	_____	_____
Total HRD program costs	$ _____	$ _____
	(Option 1)	(Option 2)

Exhibit 28. Benefit Analysis Worksheet.

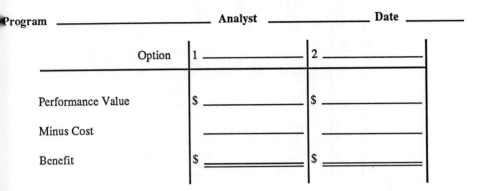

Note: Circle your choice of option.

Exhibit 29. Performance Value Worksheet.

Note that performance units and time units for all options must remain consistent throughout the forecast.

Program _Delivery Service_   **Analyst** _R.E.S._   **Date** _6/20/88_

	Option name	1 _Unstructured_	2 _Structured_
Data required for calculations:			
(a) What **unit** of work performance are you measuring?		_Delivered Papers (DP)_ unit name	_Delivered Papers (DP)_ unit name
(b) What is the performance goal per worker/work group at the **end** of the HRD program?		700 _DP_ / _Wk._ no. units / time	700 _DP_ / _Wk._ no. units / time
(c) What is the performance per worker/work group at the **beginning** of the HRD program?		600 _DP_ / _Wk._ no. units / time	600 _DP_ / _Wk._ no. units / time
(d) What **dollar value** is assigned to each performance unit?		$ _.50_ / unit	$ _.50_ / unit
(e) What is the **development time** required to reach the expected performance level?		4 _Wks._ no. time	1 _Wk._ no. time
(f) What is the **evaluation period**? (Enter the longest time (e) of all options being considered.)		4 _Wks._ no. time	4 _Wks._ no. time
(g) How many workers/work groups will **participate** in the HRD program?		_100_ no. workers/groups	_100_ no. workers/groups

Calculations to determine net performance value:

	650	DP		650	DP
	no.	units		no.	units
(h) Will worker/work group produce **usable units** during the HRD program? If no, enter -0-. If yes, enter known performance rate or calculate average performance rate. [(b + c)/2]					
(i) What total units per worker/work group will be produced during the **development time**? (h x e)	2,600 no. of units			650 no. of units	
(j) How many units will be produced per worker/work group during the **evaluation period**? {[(f – e) x b] + i}	2,600 no. of units			2,750 no. of units	
(k) What will be the value of the worker's/work group's performance during the **evaluation period**? (j x d)	$ 1,300			$ 1,375	
(l) What is the **performance value gain** per worker/work group? [k – (c x d x f)]	$ 100			$ 175	
(m) What is the **total performance value gain** for all workers/work groups? (l x g)	$ 10,000 (Option 1)			$ 17,500 (Option 2)	

Exhibit 30. Cost Analysis Worksheet.

Program ___Delivery Service___   Analyst ___R.E.S.___   Date ___6/20/88___

Option name	1 _Unstructured_	2 _Structured_
Analysis:		
Needs assessment		
Work analysis		80
Proposal to management		
Other ___		
Other ___		
Design:		
General HRD program design		
Specific HRD program design		
Other ___		
Other ___		
Development:		
Draft and prototype		120
Pilot test and revise		
Production and duplication		20
Other ___		
Other ___		
Implement:		
Program management		
Program delivery		
Participant costs		
Other _(prizes)_		100
Other _(rent)_		200
Evaluation:		
Program evaluation and report		40
Performance follow-up		
Other ___		
Other ___		
Total HRD program costs	$ ___	$ ___ 560
	(Option 1)	(Option 2)

Exhibit 31. Benefit Analysis Worksheet.

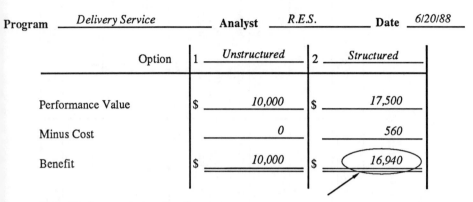

Program ___*Delivery Service*___ Analyst ___*R.E.S.*___ Date ___*6/20/88*___

	Option	1 *Unstructured*	2 *Structured*
Performance Value		$ 10,000	$ 17,500
Minus Cost		0	560
Benefit		$ 10,000	$ 16,940

Note: Circle your choice of option.

Figure 6. Performance-Time Graph.

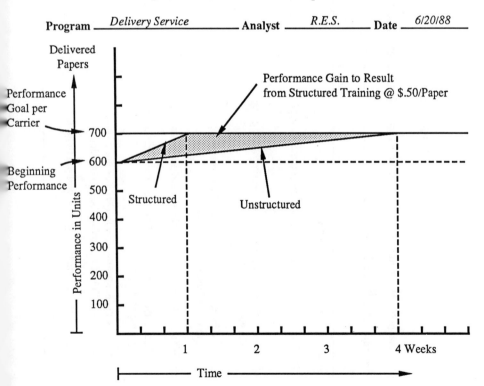

Program ___*Delivery Service*___ Analyst ___*R.E.S.*___ Date ___*6/20/88*___

Exhibit 32. Performance Value Worksheet.

Note that performance units and time units for all options <u>must remain consistent</u> throughout the forecast.

Program _Skill Training_   **Analyst** _A. Jacobson_   **Date** _4/10/88_

Option name	1 OJT & Manual	2 Factory School
Data required for calculations:		
(a) What unit of work performance are you measuring?	_Parts (Pts.)_ unit name	_Parts (Pts.)_ unit name
(b) What is the performance goal per worker/work group at the **end** of the HRD program?	_60_ no. _Pts._ / _Day_ units / time	_60_ no. _Pts._ / _Day_ units / time
(c) What is the performance per worker/work group at the **beginning** of the HRD program?	_0_ no. _Pts._ / _Day_ units / time	_0_ no. _Pts._ / _Day_ units / time
(d) What **dollar value** is assigned to each performance unit?	$ _10_ / unit	$ _10_ / unit
(e) What is the **development time** required to reach the expected performance level?	_30_ no. _Days_ time	_4_ no. _Days_ time
(f) What is the **evaluation period**? (Enter the longest time (e) of all options being considered.)	_30_ no. _Days_ time	_30_ no. _Days_ time
(g) How many workers/work groups will participate in the HRD program?	_3_ no. ⟨workers⟩/groups	_3_ no. ⟨workers⟩/groups

Calculations to determine net performance value:

	30 Pts. / units		0 Pts. / units	
	no.		no.	
(h) Will worker/work group produce usable units during the HRD program? If no, enter -0-. If yes, enter known performance rate or calculate average performance rate. [(b + c)/2]	30		0	
(i) What total units per worker/work group will be produced during the **development time**? (h x e)	900 no. of units		0 no. of units	
(j) How many units will be produced per worker/work group during the **evaluation period**? $\{[(f - e) \times b] + i\}$	900 no. of units		1560 no. of units	
(k) What will be the value of the worker's/work group's performance during the evaluation period? (j x d)	$ 9,000		$ 15,600	
(l) What is the performance value gain per worker/work group? [k – (c x d x f)]	$ 9,000		$ 15,600	
(m) What is the **total performance value gain** for all workers/work groups? (l x g)	$ 27,000 (Option 1)		$ 46,800 (Option 2)	

Exhibit 33. Cost Analysis Worksheet.

Program _Skill Training_   **Analyst** _A. Jacobson_   **Date** _4/10/88_

	Option name 1 _OJT & Manual_	2 _Factory School_
Analysis:		
Needs assessment		
Work analysis		
Proposal to management		
Other _____		
Other _____		
Design:		
General HRD program design		
Specific HRD program design		
Other _____		
Other _____		
Development:		
Draft and prototype		
Pilot test and revise		
Production and duplication		
Other _____		
Other _____		
Implement:		
Program management		
Program delivery _(factory school fees)_		6,000
Participant costs		
Other _____		
Other _____		
Evaluation:		
Program evaluation and report		
Performance follow-up		
Other _____		
Other _____		
Total HRD program costs	$ 0	$ 6,000
	(Option 1)	(Option 2)

Exhibit 34. Benefit Analysis Worksheet.

Program _____ *Skill Training* _____ Analyst _____ *A. Jacobson* _____ Date ___ *4/10/88*

Option	1 *OJT & Manual*	2 *Factory School*
Performance Value	$ 27,000	$ 46,800
Minus Cost	0	6,000
Benefit	$ 27,000	$ (40,800)

Note: Circle your choice of option.

Figure 7. Performance-Time Graph.

Program _____ *Skill Training* _____ Analyst _____ *A. Jacobson* _____ Date ___ *4/10/88*

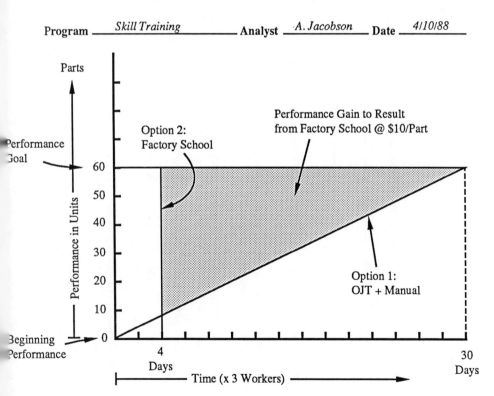

Exhibit 35. Performance Value Worksheet.

Note that performance units and time units for all options <u>must remain consistent</u> throughout the forecast.

Program __Management Development__   Analyst __G. Geroy__   Date __8/1/88__

Option name	1 __Mgt. Institute__	2 __Vendor__	3 __Coaching__
Data required for calculations:			
(a) What unit of work performance are you measuring?	Retained Engineers (R.E.) — unit name	Retained Engineers (R.E.) — unit name	Retained Engineers (R.E.) — unit name
(b) What is the performance goal per worker/work group at the **end** of the HRD program?	$\dfrac{4}{\text{no.}}\ \dfrac{R.E.}{\text{units}}\Big/\dfrac{Yr.}{\text{time}}$	$\dfrac{4}{\text{no.}}\ \dfrac{R.E.}{\text{units}}\Big/\dfrac{Yr.}{\text{time}}$	$\dfrac{4}{\text{no.}}\ \dfrac{R.E.}{\text{units}}\Big/\dfrac{Yr.}{\text{time}}$
(c) What is the performance per worker/work group at the **beginning** of the HRD program?	$\dfrac{0}{\text{no.}}\ \dfrac{R.E.}{\text{units}}\Big/\dfrac{Yr.}{\text{time}}$	$\dfrac{0}{\text{no.}}\ \dfrac{R.E.}{\text{units}}\Big/\dfrac{Yr.}{\text{time}}$	$\dfrac{0}{\text{no.}}\ \dfrac{R.E.}{\text{units}}\Big/\dfrac{Yr.}{\text{time}}$
(d) What **dollar value** is assigned to each performance unit?	$ __75,000__ / unit	$ __75,000__ / unit	$ __75,000__ / unit
(e) What is the **development time** required to reach the expected performance level?	$\dfrac{.04}{\text{no.}}\ \dfrac{Yr.}{\text{time}}$	$\dfrac{.50}{\text{no.}}\ \dfrac{Yr.}{\text{time}}$	$\dfrac{.83}{\text{no.}}\ \dfrac{Yr.}{\text{time}}$
(f) What is the **evaluation period**? (Enter the longest time (e) of all options being considered.)	$\dfrac{1}{\text{no.}}\ \dfrac{Yr.}{\text{time}}$	$\dfrac{1}{\text{no.}}\ \dfrac{Yr.}{\text{time}}$	$\dfrac{1}{\text{no.}}\ \dfrac{Yr.}{\text{time}}$
(g) How many workers/work groups will participate in the HRD program?	1 — no. workers/(groups)	1 — no. workers/(groups)	1 — no. workers/(groups)

Calculations to determine net performance value:

	Option 1		Option 2		Option 3	
	no.	R.E. units	no.	R.E. units	no.	R.E. units
(h) Will worker/work group produce usable units during the HRD program? If no, enter -0-. If yes, enter known performance rate or calculate average performance rate. [(b + c)/2]						
(i) What total units per worker/work group will be produced during the **development time**? (h x e)	0 no. of units		1 no. of units		1.66 no. of units	
(j) How many units will be produced per worker/work group during the **evaluation period**? {[(f − e) x b] + i}	3.84 no. of units		3 no. of units		2.34 no. of units	
(k) What will be the value of the worker's/work group's performance during the evaluation period? (j x d)	$ 288,000		$ 225,000		$ 175,500	
(l) What is the performance value gain per worker/work group? [k − (c x d x f)]	$ 288,000		$ 225,000		$ 175,500	
(m) What is the **total performance value gain** for all workers/work groups? (l x g)	$ 288,000 (Option 1)		$ 225,000 (Option 2)		$ 175,500 (Option 3)	

Exhibit 36. Cost Analysis Worksheet.

Program _Management Development_   Analyst _G. Geroy_   Date _8/1/88_

Option name	1 _Mgt. Institute_	2 _Vendor_	3 _Coaching_
Analysis:			
Needs assessment			10,000
Work analysis			5,000
Proposal to management			
Other _(materials: needs assessment)_			700
Other _(materials: work analysis)_			350
Design:			
General HRD program design			
Specific HRD program design			
Other _(materials)_			350
Other			
Development:			
Draft and prototype			
Pilot test and revise			
Production and duplication			1,050
Other			
Other			
Implement:			
Program management ⎫			
Program delivery ⎬	100,000	150,000	
Participant costs ⎭			
Other _(materials)_			3,500
Other			
Evaluation:			
Program evaluation and report			5,000
Performance follow-up			
Other			1,050
Other			
Total HRD program costs	$ 100,000	$ 150,000	$ 27,000
	(Option 1)	(Option 2)	(Option 3)

Exhibit 37. Benefit Analysis Worksheet.

Program _Management Development_   Analyst _G. Geroy_   Date _8/1/88_

Option	1 _Mgt. Institute_	2 _Vendor_	3 _Coaching_
Performance Value	$ 288,000	$ 225,000	$ 175,500
Minus Cost	100,000	150,000	27,000
Benefit	$ 188,000	$ 75,000	$ 148,500

Note: Circle your choice of option.

Figure 8. Performance-Time Graph.

Program _Management Development_ Analyst _G. Geroy_ Date _8/1/88_

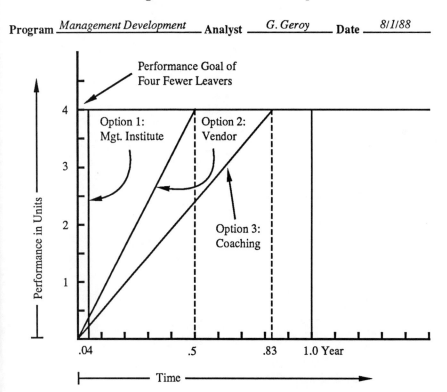

✦✦✦✦✦✦✦✦✦✦✦✦✦✦✦✦✦✦✦✦✦✦✦✦✦✦✦✦✦✦✦✦✦✦✦✦✦✦

Using a Personal Computer as an Aid in Forecasting

In the text we have presented the theory and method required to forecast the financial benefit of HRD. The basic forecasting model is supported by three different worksheets. These worksheets serve as practical job aids to ease the forecasting task. Although the Performance Value Worksheet, the Cost Analysis Worksheet, and the Benefit Analysis Worksheet are not difficult to use, the computer can help to simplify the forecasting process even further. For this reason we have developed a computer program as an additional aid for forecasting. It (1) contains the three worksheets, (2) asks the right questions, (3) calculates the numbers for you, (4) prints out your forecasts, and (5) even makes forecasting fun!

The Forecasting Financial Benefits of Human Resource Development Computer Program is a tool for readers of this book and for those who wish to gain additional efficiency in carrying out their forecasting work. The program is designed to run on IBM and IBM-compatible computers. It is written in BASICA (Advanced Basic).

What the Computer Program Does

The computer program has options and features. The options, which are in the form of a menu, allow you to choose from the following:

- Full analysis, including performance values, costs, and benefits
- Performance value analysis only

- Cost analysis only
- Benefit analysis only

Several features appear in all options. These include the ability to name your HRD option and to have that name or names appear on the screen, the ability to escape the menu option and computer program at any time, and the ability to include your own HRD program-specific header on the computer screen. This will help you keep from getting lost while you travel from screen to screen doing your analysis. The computer does all the mathematical calculations for you. The program also allows you to compare four HRD program options within a single forecast.

The full analysis starts with performance value analysis and then automatically moves on to cost analysis and finally to benefit analysis.

Performance value analysis only can be selected as a stand-alone computer program option. The set elements of performance valuing are maintained in the analysis process, and the computer will print the core data without the calculations.

Cost analysis only can also be selected as a stand-alone activity. The computer program presents the basic Cost Analysis Worksheet and offers the opportunity to develop and retain a customized version of this worksheet. In this way you can have a Cost Analysis Worksheet that matches the cost-recording system of your organization. The basic and customized Cost Analysis Worksheets are used to collect cost information.

The benefit analysis only simply subtracts costs from performance values. The data may be entered, saved, and printed out. In the full analysis option the computer program automatically computes the benefit analysis.

The Forecasting Financial Benefits of Human Resource Development Computer Program is *not* an instructional program. It does *not* teach the financial benefit forecasting method. Rather, it is a job aid for the knowledgeable forecaster.

How to Operate the Program

The written directions for operating the computer program are limited to booting the program. Once the program is functioning, the specific operating instructions appear on the computer screen. The start-up instructions are as follows:

1. At DOS prompt, load BASICA.
2. Once BASICA is operating, use the command load "pv" followed by a carriage return. At OK prompt, enter RUN.
3. Choose the preferred calculation option from the menu and then follow the directions on the screen.

Ordering Your Computer Program

The Forecasting Financial Benefits of Human Resource Development Computer Program, by James H. Sleezer, is available from Jossey-Bass Inc., Publishers, 350 Sansome Street, San Francisco, California 94104-1310 (telephone: [415] 433-1767). Call or write to obtain current prices and ordering information.

Bibliography

Carkhuff, R. R. *Sources of Human Productivity.* Amherst, Mass.: Human Resource Development Press, 1983.

Carnevale, A. P. *Human Capital: A High-Yield Corporate Investment.* Alexandria, Va.: American Society for Training and Development, 1983.

Craig, R. L. (ed.). *Training and Development Handbook.* (3rd ed.) New York: McGraw-Hill, 1987.

Cullen, G., Sisson, G., Sawzin, S., and Swanson, R. "Training, What's it Worth?" *Training and Development Journal,* 1976, *30* (8), 12–20.

Flamholtz, E. G. *Human Resource Accounting: Advances in Concepts, Methods, and Applications.* (2nd ed.) San Francisco: Jossey-Bass, 1985.

Geroy, G. D., and Swanson, R. A. "Forecasting Training Costs and Benefits in Industry." *Journal of Epsilon Pi Tau,* 1984, *10* (2), 15–19.

Gilbert, T. F. *Human Competence.* New York: McGraw-Hill, 1978.

Harless, J. *An Ounce of Analysis Is Worth a Pound of Objectives.* Boulder, Colo.: Marlin Press, 1971.

Harrison, M. I. *Diagnosing Organizations.* Beverly Hills, Calif.: Sage, 1987.

Head, G. E. *Training Cost Analysis.* Boulder, Colo.: Marlin Press, 1985.

Kaufman, R. "Assessing Needs." In *Introduction to Performance Technology.* Washington, D.C.: National Society of Performance and Instruction, 1986.

Kearsley, G. *Costs, Benefits, and Productivity in Training Systems.* Reading, Mass.: Addison-Wesley, 1982.

Kusy, M. E., Jr. *The Effects of Types of Training Evaluation on Support of Training Among Corporate Managers.* St. Paul: Training and Development Research Center, University of Minnesota, 1986.

Mager, R. F. *Analyzing Performance Problems.* Belmont, Calif.: Fearon, 1970.

Mooney, M. "Process Management Technology." *National Productivity Review*, Autumn 1986, pp. 386–391.

Mosier, N. R. *Financial Analysis: A Review of the Methods and Their Application to Employee Training.* St. Paul: Training and Development Research Center, University of Minnesota, 1986.

Parker, B. L. "Evaluation in Training and Development." *Journal of Industrial Teacher Education*, 1986, *23* (2), 29–55.

Peters, T. *Thriving on Chaos.* New York: Knopf, 1987.

Phillips, J. J. *Handbook of Training Evaluation and Measurement Methods.* Houston: Gulf, 1983.

Sleezer, C. M., Swanson, R. A., and Geroy, G. D. *Validation of the Benefit-Forecasting Method: Organization Development Program to Increase Health Organization Membership.* St. Paul: Training and Development Research Center, University of Minnesota, 1985.

Spencer, L. M., Jr. *Calculating Human Resource Costs and Benefits.* New York: Wiley, 1986.

Swanson, R. A., and Geroy, G. D. "Forecasting the Economic Benefits of Training." In P. Goldstein (ed.), *The 1987 Annual: Developing Human Resources.* San Diego: University Associates, 1987.

Swanson, R. A., and Gradous, D. *Performance at Work.* New York: Wiley, 1986.

Swanson, R. A., and Gradous, D. (eds.). *Human Resources and Organizational Change.* Alexandria, Va.: ASTD Press, 1987.

Swanson, R. A., and Sleezer, C. M. "Training Effectiveness Evaluation." *Journal of European Industrial Training*, 1987, *11* (4), 7–16.

Swanson, R. A., and Sleezer, C. M. "Organization Development: What's It Worth?" *Organization Development Journal*, Spring 1988, *6* (1), 37–42.

Tichy, N. "Managing Change Strategically: The Technical,

Political, and Cultural Keys." *Organization Dynamics,* Autumn 1982, pp. 59–80.

Tribus, M. *Becoming Competitive by Building the Quality Company.* Kingsport, Tenn.: American Quality and Productivity Institute, 1985.

U.S. Bureau of the Census. *Current Population Survey.* Washington, D.C.: U.S. Department of Commerce, January 1983.

Zemke, R., and Kerlinger, T. *Figuring Things Out.* Reading, Mass.: Addison-Wesley, 1982.

Index

of, 39; performance, 12–14, 30–36, 52, 65, 79
Nonrisk takers, 136–137, 138–139

Organization development: and benefit analysis, 142–143; and performance value analysis, 64, 76–79
Orientation for HRD programs: bottom-line, 4–5; developing, 1–7

Parker, B. L., 22
Payback period model of HRD, 21
Performance appraisal methods, 98
Performance gains: in terms of quality, 28; in terms of quantity, 28; in terms of timeliness, 27
Performance goals, 33, 50; and organizational records, 44; reaching, 49–51; tram tour example, 58–62
Performance level, definition of, 29–30
Performance needs assessment, 30, 33, 65, 79
Performance unit: examples of, 42–43; value of, 30–31
Performance unit values, estimating, 47–49
Performance value, definition of, 31
Performance value analysis, 86; an approach to, 28–31; case examples of, 26–27, 29–31, 40–41, 46, 47–48, 52–53, 54; computing a, 31–37; evaluation period in, 51–62; and HRD computer program, 171–173; management consulting firm example of, 64, 79–81; manufacturing company example of, 63, 64–70; organization development example of, 64, 71, 76–79; participation in, 52; and performance description, 37–39; and performance gains, 57–62; and performance goals, 49–51; and performance levels, 28, 29–30, 43–45; public sector agency example of, 64, 82–85; service industry example of, 64, 70–75; summary of, 62; to meet performance goals, 26–

62; and total performance, 54–56; tram tour example of, 58–62; and unit levels, 28–29; and unit value, 28, 30–31, 45–49; and work performance, 52–54
Performance value worksheet, 34–35, 154–155; for delivery service, 158–159; described, 32–33; explanation of subquestions in, 39–43; for management consulting firm, 80–81; for management development, 166–167; for manufacturing company, 66–67, 68–69; for organization development, 76–77; and performance gains, 57–62; for public sector agency, 84–85; for service industry, 72–73, 74–75; for skill training, 162–163; for tram tour, 58–62; and unit dollar values, 45–49, 50–85; using, 37–62
Performance-time graph, 153; for delivery service, 161; of HRD benefit-forecasting model, 19; for management development, 169; and performance value worksheet, 50; for skill training, 165
Personal computer forecasting program, 171–173; ease of use, 172–173; options and features, 171–172; ordering, 173
Peters, T., 26
Phillips, J. J., 22
Planned HRD programs. *See* Structured HRD programs
Production workers, 63, 64–70
Public sector agency, 64, 82–85, 103, 111–113; analysis of, 111–112; and benefit analysis, 143–144; and cost analysis, 103, 111–113; and cost analysis decisions, 113; design of HRD in, 112; evaluation of HRD in, 113; implementation of HRD in, 112–113; and performance value analysis, 64, 82–85

Quality, in performance units, 40–43